Currents & Eddies

TO

JO, BILL AND BOB

who have often joined me
in exploring many a
pleasant stream

Foreword

The stream is a living thing, restless and eager. From smallest rivulet to mighty river it moves steadily onward, its waters seeking their final destination, the sea.

In a sense it parallels life; it is impatient and must be on its way to see what lies at the end of the road. And like life, too, the stream has its moods. In spate it becomes angry, churning its roily waters, overflowing its banks and raising its voice in violent protest. But when the storm is over and the good sun again bathes the earth the flowing water recedes, slowly and gently. Now it gurgles over rocks and sings a happy song, all anger forgotten.

This is the angler's stream, the enchanted place where a true devotee can drop his fly at the head of a quiet pool, or drift it over a promising run, and by so doing find inner peace even though he takes no fish at all. For he is surrounded by nature in its many manifestations and becomes part of it.

In reading this book one might assume that it was written during the height of the season when enthusiasm ran high. Quite to the contrary, the text and pictures were prepared in the middle of winter and the endeavor had the psychological effect of shortening the time until opening day in May.

Though it is always hard to start a task, it is often more difficult to finish—especially when the subject is such a pleasant one as fishing. One writes and draws, conjuring up visions of flashing trout and arched rods. Soon the fragrance of crushed mint pervades the air, and the roar of white water is in the very room. The chill of evening creeps down and freshly caught trout are curling and sizzling in a pan over a birchwood fire.

Reminiscence naturally leads to autobiography, no matter how hard one resolves to avoid it. I find that I have not tried at all, and if an apology is needed may I say that my simple adventures are, with variations, your own. Or, if you are a beginner, you will soon experience them. For followers of the stream catch more than fish.

No attempt has been made to write about tackle or methods from a technical standpoint. The few tips I have given are quite elemental and may serve to help the newcomer to get started.

Stream fishing is a most satisfying and comforting occupation, a never-ending source of joy to those who follow it with the right spirit. It stirs the imagination and keeps alive the feeling of wonderment, without which life means little. It leads to reverence and respect.

These are the things which I have tried to set down in this little book. They are the true values.

—W. J. S.

Tubac, Arizona
May 1970

Contents

		PAGE
Foreword		ix
The Pull of the Current		1
In the Shadow of the City		21
The Bountiful Beaverkill		37
The Tools of the Trade		61
New England Chips		81
Streamside Distractions		97
River Bass		113
Quiet Eddies		125

Color Plates

FACING
PAGE

Northern Squaretail Fighting . . . . . *Frontispiece*

Brownie Somersaulting 50

Fishing the Evening Hatch 90

Rainbow in the Rips 128

Illustrations

FACING
PAGE

When the snows of winter have melted and the phoebe returns to build its nest, lucky is the lad who can spend his spare hours on a woodland trout stream 1

A hodgepodge of impressions gathered from any stream on any good day, drawn expressly to help you remember 21

When the mountain tops are cloaked with mist wraiths the angler should be on the river. This scene is typical of the Catskills 37

Though not in a class with its sea-run relative, the land-locked salmon is capable of putting up a good scrap when taken on light tackle 61

This is the thrilling moment for the dry-fly angler. The rise is more fun than the fight—especially when the trout is a husky, speckled "native" 81

An angler who fishes silently and is observant may have the good luck to come upon a vain cock grouse strutting pompously before an utterly indifferent hen . . . 97

The boss of the river is the smallmouth—a tough, hard-living, fast-fighting gent, worthy of every angler's utmost respect 113

Fly-rod artistry is built along the stretches of a small stream. An occasional session is good for every angler; it will teach him patience and humility 125

Currents & Eddies

When the snows of winter have melted and the phoebe returns to build its nest, lucky is the lad who can spend his spare hours on a woodland trout stream.

The Pull of the Current

BOYS ARE BORN WITH THE instinct of the chase in their blood. Most of them have it knocked out, either by unsympathetic parents or unfortunate circumstances. The lucky ones grow up to be sportsmen and are Earth's favored children all their days, even though, according to standards of worldly achievement, they should fail in almost everything else. In some individuals the hunting instinct is strong and unfluctuating; others have it in spells, like a siege of grippe, or lose it altogether. I have always been grateful that I was handed a double dose. For I can't remember the day when I didn't long to be afoot with rod or gun.

From earliest childhood, stories of Indians, trappers, explorers and fishermen fascinated me. I wanted desperately to have a gun and learn to shoot. But the first decade of a fellow's life is too soon—even for an air rifle. He can afford to wait. Mother compromised by buying me a small archery outfit, said to be patterned after the English longbow. I had heard tales of this famous weapon; how at Crécy and Agincourt cloth-yard shafts were sent right through a knight in armor so that they

1

came out the other side. This fascinated me. Anything powerful enough to penetrate two thicknesses of armor, plus one thickness of knight, must have been a pretty good weapon. I knew that my toy bow couldn't do anything like that, of course, but it should be strong enough for English sparrows, which were nuisances and therefore fair game. But I overlooked one point: the tackle was so crude that no two arrows would ever shoot into the same place.

Regretfully I gave up the bow in favor of the slingshot, a weapon with definite virtues in the hands of a skilled performer. I was seldom without this ingenious combination of crotch, elastic bands and leather pouch, even carrying it to the classroom, where it was occasionally lifted by a stern and coldly realistic teacher. With constant practice I was able to pink a sparrow here and there, plug bullfrogs and rid our yard permanently of marauding cats. No matter how tough an old tom might think himself, once you bounced a pebble off his rump he never came back.

Until I reached my late teens I was not allowed a real gun; so I became passionately devoted to fishing—it was a sport which let me go out and get something to bring in. Dad was sympathetic and took me with him when I was just a little tot. I can still remember our first trip. We were up at sunrise.

Dew lay heavy on the grass that May morning, and the slanting shafts of sunlight burned it off, sending streamers of mist wraiths twisting fantastically upward. Bird voices filled the air, and along the meadow path where we walked the new grass was sprinkled with adder's-tongue, anemone and violets.

My father talked about the trees, birds and other fascinating things we encountered along the way, and I drank it in hungrily. His love of nature was vast, and it was several years before I realized that fishing was, more often than not, merely an excuse to get him out in the open. For Father was not, in the ordinary sense of the term, a sportsman. A cane pole and live minnows or worms constituted his tackle; of fly-fishing or the then young sport of bait-casting he knew nothing. In his boyhood he had shot wild pigeons and an occasional prairie chicken in his native state of Wisconsin. But long before I was born he had given up the gun.

We lived on the outskirts of town, and in less than an hour had reached the river. Soon we were rigged and busily fishing. In those days one did not have long to wait for results. Every eddy and backwater seemed filled with fish of some variety, from the homely and unwanted red horse to that mighty battler, the small-mouthed black bass. But it was pan-fish in which we were chiefly interested—the beautiful bluegill, with his bright orange breast, and that ludicrous mottled fellow with the Martian eyes which text books call rock bass. To me he will always be the "redeye." And finally the handsome calico bass.

I soon learned to swing the baited hook out into the gentle current, to wait for the plucking bite of a fish, and then, when he had taken the bobber down, to throw him over my head into the bushes. It was the first page of the primer, and I was an absorbed pupil. The lessons ahead looked pleasant indeed.

All too soon the sun began to lower in the western sky, and it was time to go home. I remember vaguely a cloth flour sack heavy with pan-fish, tired legs and huge hunger as we struck the path. Suddenly Dad dropped the sack of fish and cried, "Look, look!"

I saw a chunky brownish snake a yard long with a sizable fish in its mouth, still alive and futilely twisting. Dad killed the reptile, a water snake, with the butt of his cane pole, thereby giving me my first lesson in conservation. Vivid as that incident still is, something else took place on that May evening which has gathered added meaning as the years roll along.

Crossing a bridge on the way home, we stopped a moment to look down into the clear water. A school of suckers and brook minnows fanned the current, maintaining a steady position in the stream. Leaves and chips floated slowly over them, obeying the impulse of the running water. Occasionally a fish would dart out of line, seize a bit of food, then swing back again into position.

Dad talked about the current, how it ran so steadily and smoothly and how the fish thrived under its influence by keeping their heads pointed upstream. The gist of it all was that you couldn't get anywhere by fighting nature. Of course, I was too young to realize what he meant, but already I was under the spell—as all true anglers are—of the pull of the current. The love of the stream, not only for the sport it might afford, but for its infinite beauty, its mystery and its parallel to life was surely born in me that day. A lasting spark had been kindled.

During the next three years I visited the river frequently, sometimes with my father, but oftener in the company of my schoolmates. As I grew older I would wander off alone without permission and be gone for an entire day. Though I knew that a sound scolding awaited me in the evening, the lure of the open was too much to resist. There was so much to see and to learn, and the warm weather passed so quickly!

To my conquest of the common pan-fishes—bluegills, perch and redeyes—I steadily added new members. There were suckers of several species—chief among which was the silver-and-scarlet red horse—warmouth bass, the beautiful green sunfish, bullheads and the long, snaky grass pike.

But the glory of those Indiana rivers of long ago was the black bass. In the steady, smooth flow of the Elkhart and St. Joe the smallmouth grew large and powerful. Sometimes in a clear pool I would see the huge form of an old bronzeback, lurking in the shadowy depths. These monsters would disdain my most careful offerings, though I did occasionally catch a bass a foot long.

Once I saw a fisherman land a 4-pound smallmouth on an ordinary cane pole, fishing the riffles in the St. Joe. He was using soft crawfish for bait, an irresistible lure. To see that big bass leap and make the line saw through the water set me on fire with ambition; but I was too small to wield the 16-foot bamboo pole needed to get the bait to where the big fellows lay.

On warm nights in the spring and early summer I was sometimes permitted to join a party to go "bullheadin'." That may sound like a prosaic occupation; but in case you've never done it, don't be in a hurry to judge. The bullhead leaves a lot to be desired in the way of looks, it is true. Nature played hell with him from an aesthetic standpoint—gave him a shovel

head, long whiskers, little pig eyes with a mean look and a hide the color of mud. To make it worse, she armed him with spiny fins that stab your fingers like a red-hot needle.

The bullhead, however, has his good points. On the table he's hard to beat when fried to a golden brown. And best of all, he's cooperative. Just feed him what he wants—which is a worm or a chunk of liver—and he will bite most obligingly. Furthermore, he won't even take the trouble to put up a scrap, but will meekly permit himself to be lifted up on the bank and dumped into a pail with his stupid fellows.

But it wasn't just the bullhead that lured us to the river at night. It was a hundred other things—the sound of running water, the dank sweet fragrance of moss-covered rocks, locust perfume on the air, a yellow-throated bullfrog bellowing resonantly into the darkness, the insistent challenge of the whip-poorwill. For these impressions I thank the bullhead, and am glad that I met him early.

Most of the boys with whom I fished regarded the sport as a game in a class with tops, kites or marbles—a seasonal occupation to take up and drop when they tired of it. But with me fishing was a passion, and I could never learn enough about the inhabitants of the waters, and the woods and fields that bordered them. I read every book obtainable at the library on angling, nature and life in the open. When I was ten, I got hold of Henry Van Dyke's *Little Rivers* and stumbled through much that was beyond me. But it filled me with the determination to be a fly fisherman.

In northern Indiana trout were unknown, and I had only seen pictures of the famous "speckled beauties." But these were enough to fill me with an intense desire to "whip the stream," as the books put it. One folder in particular had me starry-eyed. It was, as I recall, a publication of the Grand Rapids and Indiana Railroad. Its cover design was a plate of wet flies in full color—Professor, Brown Hackle, Parmacheene Belle, Seth Green. Queen-of-the-Waters and other patterns.

What gorgeous creations they were! Cuts in the folder showed fishermen "tied into a big one" on such romantic-sounding streams as the Little Manistee, Pine, Boardman and Jordan.

I practically lived with that precious booklet. Michigan was the Never-never land, and some day I would go there to live. How true that childhood wish would be I did not then know. But first I was to spend a summer in Minnesota.

My maternal grandmother lived in a nice old-fashioned house on the edge of the town of Rochester. It was a fascinating place, with ample grounds, flourishing garden innocent of weeds, and many thrifty fruit trees. But best of all, the Zumbro River meandered pleasantly through rolling meadow country only a short distance away. My cousins liked to fish, and they showed me the best spots for crappies, bluegills and bass soon after my arrival. Like the streams of Indiana where I had fished, the Zumbro was not over-populated with anglers in those days, and we never had any difficulty in getting a mess of pan-fish.

My cousins' father—who was my uncle Jake—was about the first real sportsman I had met. He was an enthusiastic angler who fished for bass and northern pike whenever he had spare time. To one who had known only a cane pole and cotton line, his collection of split-bamboo rods, reels, lines and lures was something to contemplate with reverence. I stared in goggle-eyed wonderment as each precious item was exhibited. And when he lent me a jointed rod, completely equipped, for my very own use, I knew that I had found the person I had been looking for. He handed me the key which could open the door.

On the near-by river I learned to cast sufficiently well to get a bait out into the current much farther than was possible with the clumsy cane pole. I experimented a little, too, with crude flies which I fashioned from yarn, chicken feathers and colored silk, tied on ringed hooks. Strangely enough, I caught some crappies. The fish in those far-off years weren't fussy—they hadn't learned the difference between a bivisible and a prismatic-hackled palmer.

Near-home fishing was fun, but the real thrill came on those rare trips to Oronoco, a long carriage drive from town, down the river. Uncle kept good horses, and he would load the surrey with tackle, baskets of food, buckets of live minnows and hellgrammites—enough supplies for a week, though we invariably returned at night. We were off at dawn, filled with anticipation which was seldom left unrewarded, for the river at Oronoco was scarcely fished.

As I look back on it now, it is difficult to believe that we came home with catches of big pike and bass that would do credit to remote wilderness regions of today. The explanation, of course, lies in the phenomenon of the motorcar. My uncle had the first Cadillac agency in Rochester, but he never took his own car far out of town. He didn't dare—the roads were too poor for anything but horse and buggy.

The rolling country of southern Minnesota took hold of me hard, and I learned to love the beautiful river which had afforded me so much pleasure. As the end of our stay approached I would sit on the stream's bank and listen to the murmur of water hurrying along through the meadows. The pull of the current was biting in deeper and deeper.

It was hard to leave such pleasant scenes, and the years have only served to heighten that feeling. I find it difficult to tear myself away from the stream, even after a long day's fishing. There is something deeply satisfying about pausing for a few moments of contemplation in the twilight, listening to the last notes of the wood thrush and watching the evening star twinkle through birch leaves.

During the next two summers we visited Minnesota again and spent some time in Wisconsin and Ohio. The Zumbro River and other streams were like old friends; so it was merely a matter of shaking hands and saying howdy. In the other two states I was a total stranger, but this caused no embarrassment, for I had already learned the technique of extracting information of the sort I wanted. Local fishermen will always tell you a little; and from there on you can improvise.

When I was twelve, my dream came true—we moved to Michigan. At first, Grand Rapids seemed like a huge city, because I had always lived in small towns where you could walk to open country in a short time. But by the process that never failed—asking questions of every one who might know anything about it—I soon learned that the situation wasn't at all hopeless. In fact, it had distinct possibilities. There was the river, for one thing, and at several points some brooks and creeks that actually had trout in them. Some of these streams could be reached by a five-cent fare on the trolley.

The Grand River, especially north of town, reminded me a lot of the streams where I had received preliminary schooling. Old friends were there—redeyes, black bass, sunfish—and I was to make new acquaintances in the form of the sheepshead, or fresh-water drum, the channel cat and several other interesting, though not important, species.

I had many exciting hours on the old river during the first two summers, but my goal had not been reached. This was, of course, fly-fishing for trout in some of the wonderful streams I had read about in that railroad booklet. But first I needed tackle. Money was hard come by in those days, and anything like a good fly rod was away beyond my reach; so I set about making one.

The public library was a godsend, with its stacks of books devoted to sport, nature and life in the open. There was a work that described the making of a rod from butt to tip, and I soon had it practically memorized. Evenings after school and rainy holidays were devoted to planing, scraping and sanding strips of seasoned hickory to the proper taper. A set of cheap nickel shouldered ferrules and reel seat of the same material constituted the hardware. The grip was made of sumac. Guides were whipped on, wrappings completed and two coats of spar varnish applied. When I jointed her up and strung a cheap enameled line through the guides, pride popped from every pore.

It doesn't take much imagination to sense what that old rod was like. By the most charitable estimate its weight must have been 12 ounces. To be strictly realistic, that is three-quarters of a pound—quite a burden for the wrist of a rather slight boy of twelve! Hickory is not only heavy, but slow and logy, and a rod made of it is probably the worst instrument that could be conceived for propelling a fly. It is little wonder that my attempts at casting were delayed until I could get a split-bamboo rod, and every cent earned in spare time was saved toward that end.

But the old hickory stick made a noble bait rod. Using a live minnow, night-crawler or spoon, I could hook and lick the toughest bass or channel cat in short order. It was as durable as a locust fence post and practically as tough, capable of standing anything short of blows from an ax. The tip, being of fairly fine diameter—considering the material—soon took a permanent set. I was forced to make a concession to pride by buying a cheap split-bamboo tip. This improved the action of the wand—if it could truthfully be called action—and still left it two-thirds hand-made.

In my early teens the ever-annoying problem of transportation became magically solved. I acquired a bicycle and soon had sought out every stream within pumping distance of home. Strawberry and Mill Creek, north of town, afforded me many fine days and some good catches of trout. But my special delight was a small brook about five miles to the south of where we lived. This was Laraway Creek, named after the family through whose property a long strip of the stream flowed.

The farm was called Walnut Place, because it had over a

hundred of the fine old nut trees scattered over its rolling acres. "Aunt" Belle and "Uncle" Barney welcomed me, and I would often spend week-ends with them, roaming about the plowed fields looking for arrowheads, trapping muskrats in the fall and fishing for trout during the open season.

Laraway Creek differed from many of the trout streams I fished in that it was a meadow brook throughout most of its short course. It came from a large spring on the side of a hill, and the water was noted for its crystal clearness. The brook trout that lived in it were, as might be expected, exceedingly shy. Fishing such a stream was good discipline for an impetuous youngster. The cautious stalking tactics which have served me so well on many a hard-to-fish stream were learned there.

The longed-for split-bamboo fly rod was finally obtained, and it marked a mile-stone in my life. It was an Abbey and Imbrie, 9 feet in length, weighing 5½ ounces. The retail price was 18 dollars, but since I had a job in a sporting-goods store, working after school and Saturdays, I was able to get it at a wholesale price.

Other equipment was acquired, a little at a time—one of the famous old Featherlight reels, a Saline enameled line, good honest gut leaders and a few of the exquisite but expensive Orvis wet flies. Among the killing patterns were Cahill, Brown Hackle, Stone Fly, Hare's Ear, Wickham's Fancy and, above all, McGinty. These flies are all effective today in many parts of the East, as well as the mid-West. Just last spring young Bill wrote me from college, asking for some McGintys—said the trout in New Hampshire were eating them up, and none could be obtained there.

I did not abjure bait-fishing and become a convert to the ranks of the purists. But the sport to be had with the artificial fly became more apparent on each successive trip. With the affluence which came through spare-time work, those distant fair fields of which I had long dreamed were opened up. Loose change, jingling in a trouser pocket, could be translated into railroad tickets—on that same G. R. and I. whose folder had held forth such promise. Or on the Pere Marquette, which traversed some fine trout country.

Soon I made the acquaintance of several productive streams, all of them good fly water, and progressed slowly. Two of my favorites were at Edgerton—Stegman and Burch Creeks. In those days they were able to maintain a steady supply of trout with only the stocking of fry by the state, once a year. Any average day would yield a creel of fine fish, mostly brook trout, with a few rainbows or an occasional brown. The latter two species were beginning to become popular. The Michigan length limit was 7 inches, but 12-inch trout were not uncommon, and on lucky days the creel would contain a 15-incher.

It was on Stegman Creek that I first made the discovery that flies can often be deadlier than bait. Late one afternoon I was fishing through deep woods, a short distance behind another fellow. He was plunking a worm in ahead of him and clumsily splashing through good water, putting fish down. I sat down to let things rest and allow the trout to settle.

In a few moments a trout rose in a run through which the fisherman had waded. Putting on a six-foot leader and single No. 10 wet fly, I hooked and landed a good trout. Then, following less than ten minutes behind the worm-fisherman, I took eight or ten trout, the largest of which was 14 inches. I met him at the station that evening, and he complained bitterly that the creek was fished out!

Edgerton was my favorite spot, and I fished its two streams for several years, sometimes alone, but often in the company of my old partner, Espy Stanton. Other streams in that general locality gave us good sport, too—a brook at Rockford, Whitney Creek, Cedar Creek at Cedar Springs and, farther along the line, Bigelow Creek at Newaygo.

One of the pleasantest streams I ever waded was the White River, above White Cloud. It was teeming with beautiful native brook trout, and the upper reaches lay in a quite primitive country, reached only by a long hike from the railroad station. Shortly before leaving Michigan, I made a memorable trip to this charming place.

It was late in September, and the shooting and fishing seasons overlapped. I hiked to the cabin of a friend, up on the headwaters of the river, and spent the night. At dawn I was off, equipped with fly rod, tackle and 16-gauge double gun, in a canvas case, slung over my shoulder.

Fishing downstream with wet flies, I took a nice creel of trout and garnished them with several jack-snipe and a pair of green-winged teal, which I picked up en route. Near the old

Northern Light Dam, I made camp at noon and fried freshly caught trout for my meal. The ashes of many camp-fires have been left in widely scattered places since that day, but none holds fonder memories.

In 1912, I believe, a unique book was added to the American sporting library. It was "Practical Dry-fly Fishing," by Emelyn M. Gill. I got hold of a copy a year or two later and studied it with fervor. It described the English method of fishing a floating fly as applied to our streams. I was enthralled and eager to try out the principles, but no tackle was available in town. So I obtained a catalog from an English house, W. and J. Cummins of Bishop Auckland, and sent them a small order.

To this day, I have never seen more beautiful flies than those dainty little uprights, tied on Hall's turned-up eyed hooks. One tiny Black Gnat, tied on a No. 20 hook, was so exquisite that I couldn't bear to use it. I still have it, in the original black-enameled box which came from England so many years ago.

The principle of dry-fly fishing centers around upstream casting, with a lure which floats on the surface. Old-time wet-fly fishermen invariably worked downstream and cast their feathered lures—two or three on the leader—slightly quartering to the current, then dragged them back with little jerks by twitching the wrist and retrieving line with the left hand. I started out this way, but on one of my trips to the Pine River I met a fine old gentleman by the name of Randall.

"Dad," as he was affectionately known, was then near eighty, but he was lithe and agile and possessed the enthusiasm of a boy. He made beautiful rods, splitting the cane by hand, calipering the strips, even making the metal fittings. It was Dad Randall who first told me that my rod was too soft, and therefore inefficient. In a day before the virtues of backbone had become generally recognized he had figured it out for himself.

It was Dad, also, who had discovered that a deadly way to fish a wet fly is upstream, with a short line and single fly. He taught me this trick, and I mastered it on the Pine, one of Michigan's loveliest streams. In fact, this resourceful and ingenious old angler had been—from a standpoint of tackle and tactics—using the dry-fly method for years, with one exception: his lure traveled just under the surface, instead of floating. Having learned his method, it was easy for me to shift to dry-fly fishing and grasp at least the rudiments of the art when the sport was young in this country.

One of the first good fish I ever took on a floater fell to a tiny No. 16 Queen-of-the-Waters, in the pool below the old mill-dam at Edgerton. It was the evening hour so loved by fly fishermen, when the heat of the day had passed and a myriad of aquatic insects danced over the surface of the gently flowing water. Trout were feeding regularly, and I went into action, laying a wet fly as delicately as I could over rise after rise. But though I changed flies several times and tried varied methods of retrieving them, the fish would not pay the slightest heed.

Remembering the dainty dry flies, I rigged up with the little 16 Queen tied to a drawn gut leader, greased a few yards of the line and cast again. Almost instantly the floater was taken, and I had a real battle before bringing to net a very fat and beautiful brook trout over 14 inches in length. Several other nice fish were taken in the next half hour. It was a convincing demonstration of what the dry-fly method can do under favorable conditions.

As so often happens, enthusiasm was away out ahead of knowledge and experience. I tied some rather clumsy dry flies and originated a few patterns, imitating natural insects. I even went so far as to make drawings of them and write a descriptive text, submitting the "illustrated article" to a sporting magazine national in scope. They bought and published it, which didn't surprise me at the time, but amazes me now. That feeble wheeze appeared in print as long ago as 1915, making me, at the advanced age of 19, an author, illustrator and dry-fly angler —so I fondly believed.

During the following two years I devoted all of my spare time to fishing, shooting on the uplands and marshes, and drawing game birds and fish. I was seriously considering the study of art as a profession when an event took place which called a halt to my plans. The United States declared war on the Central Powers in April, 1917.

Like all young fellows, I was restless, but obligations kept me at home until cold weather. Late in the fall I took a long hunt through the hill country west of Edgerton, returning with three grouse and a cottontail. Then, like Stephen Foster's old darky, I "hung up de fiddle an' de bow" and enlisted in the United States Naval Reserve force.

After being discharged from active duty in 1919, I returned to Michigan for the summer, fished some of the old streams, then left for good to go east, study art and learn something about the waters of the Appalachian system. My education was beginning in more ways than one.

A hodgepodge of impressions gathered from any stream on any good day, drawn expressly to help you remember.

In the Shadow of the City

TO ONE ACCUSTOMED TO HAVING the open countryside as a near neighbor—a street-car ride or a moderate pedal on a bicycle away—New York seemed a pretty formidable place. I knew, of course, that I had gone east to seek a job and to study; but there is a limit to what a fellow can do in the pure realm of labor. When spring broke, as it was bound to do after a fashion even in the city canyons of Gotham, how was I to answer its summons?

Robins and song sparrows would announce the age-old miracle on their way through Central Park, and I, sitting disconsolately on a bench, would wonder how I was to escape from the endless miles of brick and concrete and milling masses. My partner in Michigan had warned me about it. The "effete East," he called it, and solemnly cautioned me that if I were to attempt it nothing but disaster would be my lot. I would soon become pallid and lose the use of my muscles, as did all city people, and be unable to wade a trout stream or hunt through a grouse cover. But these dire predictions never materialized.

I arrived in New York in August of 1919, and, after a preliminary month or so of making adjustments, settled down to the only thing I knew—selling tackle in a big sporting-goods house. I drew at night, attending a class at the Art Students League. I asked questions constantly, following a childhood custom. Before the autumn was over, I had shot some grouse and woodcock, and learned enough about angling possibilities within a reasonable distance to make me restless all winter. This made me very happy, because it was a normal condition and I knew that I wasn't going to rot.

At this point, discretion would indicate that I had better inform the reader of my general intentions before he drops the book in disgust, thinking that he has been tricked into buying an autobiography. The only purpose I have in writing of my own experiences is to tell something about the path I have followed in becoming a sportsman. Now, there is nothing unique about that path. It parallels the journey of every one who has seriously adopted the rod or gun, whether from childhood or as an adult avocation. Each has something to teach to another, even if it is only a new leader knot. I hope that the novice may pick up a kink here and there as he goes along; the old-timer will bear with me, for my adventures are, with slight variations, his own.

It would be an exaggeration to say that Westchester County in those days even remotely resembled a wild country. It didn't. The real-estate agents started working on it, no doubt, shortly after 42nd Street became known as uptown in Manhattan, and great estates slowly developed. More land is being parked up yearly, yet the numbers of game birds, animals and fish within a couple of hours' train ride of Grand Central Terminal is incredible. It is also encouraging to a city-locked person with sporting blood, once he finds the key.

For ten years I snooped around the hills, valleys, swamps and streams of Westchester, sallying occasionally into Putnam and Dutchess Counties. None of this country is more than one hundred miles from the city, and most of it is under fifty. Some of the finest catches of trout I ever made, including large individual fish, came from streams located within what I call the shadow of the city. And these waters are still yielding sport.

How is this possible? There are two principal reasons: an unusually fortunate network of streams and lakes; and faithful, sustained work on the part of an organization that has become a model for sportsmen's groups—the Southern New York Fish and Game Association.

It was my good fortune to be present at the founding of the Association in 1919 and to meet many fine sportsmen who were generous with the information I so hungrily sought. I lived in White Plains, headquarters of the organization, and soon made the acquaintance of such streams as the East and West Branches of the Croton, the outlet and inlet streams of Titicus, Cross River Outlet, Byram River and many others.

My interest had centered almost exclusively on the dry fly, and these waters were ideally suited to it. The Michigan streams were natural waterways for the most part, but in the metropolitan area it was different. Suitable valleys along original small rivers had been filled by impounding the waters at certain points to form a chain of reservoirs—part of the vast Croton watershed, which acts as a reserve water supply for New York City.

One of the most interesting streams for the fly-fisherman, for example, is that strip of the West Branch of the Croton which is the outlet of West Branch Reservoir. It flows through several miles of forested land, tumbles down through rocky country and empties into Hemlock Reservoir. There are several small but beautiful waterfalls, many long glassy pools, and much pocket water where a dry-fly man may exercise such skill as he possesses. And generally it won't be enough, for the West Branch is not only the home of sophisticated trout, but is a mean devil to wade.

This fascinating stream gave us excellent sport, when conditions were right, in the early 'twenties, and in spite of vastly increased angler traffic in recent years it continues to produce. So do all of these much-hammered watershed streams, and there is a definite reason.

The once-natural rivers of this area are now really flowages, connecting and linking together large and deep reservoirs. Trout planted in the streams have access to these artificial lakes, and there they may grow to prodigious size, thriving in the waters which are rich in plankton. Furthermore, there is a fairly steady flow maintained, so that, even during the heat of summer cold water from the reservoirs runs through the channels of the various streams, and fishing may be had when in natural rivers and brooks trout are panting for breath in a semi-parboiled state.

Twenty years ago Dr. Ralph Warren Sweetser and I made a trip to the West Branch in mid-June to carry out an important commission. My son Bill had just been born, and his mother and he were still in the hospital. It was a little too soon for the young fellow to enjoy broiled trout, but she had expressed a desire for that item—which, of course, is definitely off the track on hospital menus.

We took the train to Brewster, had a fellow drive us over to a point well up above Hemlock, and spent the day fishing upstream toward Krafts; "Cheeseburg" was Doc's droll name for the place. There was a hatch of small gingers on the water, and trout were feeding on every slick and riffle. It made little difference what we used; we hit fish everywhere and with anything.

A big fan-wing Royal Coachman handed Doc a 15-inch brook trout in a long, dark pool overhung with hemlocks. He missed another rise, and we sat down to rest the fish. In ten minutes he asked me to try and, using a No. 10 fan-wing Royal, I was soon fast, landing a brookie that was a harness mate to the first one.

Not since leaving the clear, smooth reaches of the Pine in Michigan had I seen anything like that. Nor was it to be repeated again. Our creels were heavy with fine fish that evening, most of them brown trout, a few rainbows, and the balance brook trout. It was one of those rare red-letter days, and several patients at the hospital blessed the bounty of the West Branch.

In contrast, I can remember some blank trips and not a few indifferent ones, where the reward of a whole day's effort would be two or three trout. But where in the whole realm of fishing does that not hold true?

Though I deserted the metropolitan area in 1929, to leave the city for good—so I thought—I have always had a lively interest in and a rather sentimental affection for the streams that gave me so much pleasure for a full decade. Many of my friends still fish these waters each year, and from them and other sources I keep in touch with current conditions.

The history of angling in over-populated areas is usually depressing. The graph goes down violently as pressure increases. Fishermen elbow each other rudely in a vain attempt to find standing room, waiting impatiently for the truck to dump adult trout into the stream, which otherwise would be practically depleted. This is the cartoonist's version and, unfortunately, in some cases it's virtually true. But not in many Westchester streams, for the very good reason that there is too much water. If trout don't like the company, they can depart into the lakes—and frequently they do.

The proof of this lies in the record, for in the past decade or so more big trout have been taken from Westchester County than at any other concentrated area in the East. There is only one exception, and that is Catharine Creek, in the Finger Lakes region. First Prize brown trout in a recent *Field &*

Stream Annual Fishing Contest came from Rye Lake—about twenty-five miles from Central Park. It weighed 16½ pounds! Many rainbows scaling over 10 and 12 pounds are taken in the reservoirs, and in the connecting flowages a lucky fisherman may occasionally tie into 4- and 5-pounders.

If the picture is so rosy, why, then, do we hear so much condemnation of near-city fishing? The reason can perhaps be

best illustrated with a story. It came from Ted Townsend, noted game warden and sportsman, whose connection with the affairs of stream and woodland in Westchester County is renowned. If anyone has seen life in one of its interesting facets—that of game protector—Ted is the man. Many of the stories of this noted raconteur are exceedingly funny. A few have an undercurrent of pathos, like this:

While patrolling upper Kensico Reservoir one day in the

summer, he spotted a fisherman sitting on the bank. Going over to check, he found a middle-aged Italian, with his head in his hands, looking very glum.

"Any luck, Tony?" Ted said.

"Luck?" the dejected one replied, "me, I gotta onlee da bad luck. All day I'm sit here, but da feesh she's no bite. No eata da beautee-ful bait; fella in da store say she's sure catch. One dollaire I pay. Look. I am dees-a-goost."

Whereupon he hauled up a five-gang underwater plug which had been resting on the bottom in ten feet of water for hours on end!

That, of course, is an extreme case, but an inspection of the fishermen along any typical watershed stream is pretty apt to turn up some incredible rigs. Much of the tackle used is too heavy and clumsy. I have seen fellows splashing away with bass fly rods and No. 6 Parmacheene Belle or Silver Doctor flies, coupled on to double gut leaders. These, of course, were beginners, without guidance, groping their way about in the dark.

Many newcomers use bait tackle and worms, thinking it the most certain way of obtaining a mess of trout. It decidedly isn't, except possibly after a rain, when the water is roiled. Even then a man who is clever with a bucktail or a streamer can generally beat a worm fisherman. For these are civilized trout, sophisticated to a high degree.

Probably the majority of fishermen who visit the streams near New York have very fair tackle and can handle a fly well enough. Yet it is safe to say that not many of them make consistently good catches. The fish are undoubtedly there. Why, then, do they fail? For several reasons—they do not know enough about the habits of trout; they are unobserving; they are, above all, unadaptable. A really good angler is like a good hound. Drop him off in a strange country and let him take a turn around; he'll soon catch scent and be perfectly at home. I can't think of a better illustration of this than the story Ladd Plumley told me.

Plumley, one of the best fly-fishermen this country ever saw, was for many years Fishing Editor of *Field & Stream*. He decided to retire in 1926, and I took his place. Before leaving for the West he told me that I would be asked fishing questions by many types of people and that I should take them all seriously, even though the queries might seem elemental. And sometimes, he said, I might learn more than I taught.

Then he told me about the Englishman who came into the office one Friday afternoon and wanted to locate some first-class trout fishing near New York.

"First-class trout fishing—think of that!" Plumley said with a chuckle. "Well, you know what fishing is like around here. I didn't want to mislead the man, but he seemed so earnest that I sort of got carried away.

"I talked to him for about an hour and sent him away happy. But after he had left I felt pangs of guilt and really began to worry. For I had revealed my pet stretch of stream, told him how to get there—even what flies I generally used.

"I've fished this place for years, and once in a while I do get a nice fish. They're in there, all right, but, man, are they shy! I felt that a stranger wouldn't have a ghost of a chance. Whatever impelled me to tell him about it I don't know.

"Well, sir, bright and early on Monday morning he showed up smiling like a kid.

" 'What luck?' I asked with fear and trembling.

" 'Ripping, perfectly ripping!' he replied. 'I found everything as you said. A beautiful stream, sir—it worked out wonderfully, even to the flies you recommended.'

" 'Did—did you get any trout?' I stuttered.

" 'Oh, indeed,' he answered, 'half a dozen good ones. I brought back one which I'd like you to accept with my compliments.' Then he opened a package and hauled out as beautiful an 18-inch brown trout as I have seen anywhere.

"That fellow was a fisherman," Plumley concluded. "He knew the ropes and would get along anywhere. But before I found it out he certainly gave me a few bad moments."

The angler who fishes near New York—or any populous center, for that matter—must make up his mind that he is bound to face plenty of competition. Only in the wilderness can he escape it. The metropolitan fisherman does not fight crowded conditions—he learns to cope with them, and in so doing derives tremendous satisfaction from his modest successes.

Even two decades ago there were plenty of fishermen on the Westchester streams and it was difficult to find a stretch an eighth of a mile long without someone waving a rod over it, especially on week-ends. Those were the days of experiment, when the dry-fly method, as practiced in America, was comparatively young.

We were enthusiasts of an intense nature, the group of men with whom I fished, always eager to learn and to try out new ideas and theories. We regarded the near-home waters as a testing laboratory, and competition in the form of strange fishermen, popping up at our pet places, acted as extraneous bugs which had to be strained out of the mixture before the formula would work. It was excellent discipline, and every good fish creeled was a sweet prize.

Ted Townsend was—and is—one of the finest dry-fly anglers in the land. Like a true artist, he was never satisfied with the picture, and he kept changing parts here and there—a lighter rod, perhaps, or a new approach to his cast. For a period he abandoned tapered leaders and fished nine feet of 2X gut—with admirable results. When we were convinced that he had something, he'd suddenly abandon the idea and start out fresh. Such a perfectionist is never satisfied short of heaven, of course, but what a pile of fun he has!

Lou Petry, a dear old friend who has crossed the Divide, tied exquisite flies. We soon became dissatisfied with "store" flies, dainty creations though they were, because practically all of the available floaters of that time were English importations. They bore quaint names like Pale Watery Dun, Halford's Orange Upright and Tupp's Indispensable. Of course, they took fish, but they seemed just too damned precious.

We craved something more rugged; especially, we wanted counterparts of the insects to be found on our waters. Not that they would necessarily catch more trout, but they seemed to fit in better with our ideas. Fishermen are that way—especially dry-fly fishermen.

Lou spent long hours over his vise creating new patterns, some of them in imitation of insects found on the stream, others fanciful but buggy-looking. Invariably they took fish. As fast as he would tie them his admiring friends would wheedle them from him, and it was with difficulty that he could keep his own fly boxes stocked. Among his many creations were two which seemed universally successful: Petry's Orange Egg Sac and his Lemon Woodduck. These would take fish in the Beaverkill, the Westchester streams or the Adirondacks. That was a good many years ago, but every once in a while I use the patterns in odd places and find them as killing as ever.

Next to flies, rods were discussed more than any other single item of tackle. For a time such emphasis was laid on back-bone that a lot of decidedly uncomfortable rods were being fished, with the result that we are nursing sore wrists at the end of the day. Length, too, entered the picture, and we ran the gamut from $7\frac{1}{2}$ to $9\frac{1}{2}$ feet. I won't go into that now, for a separate chapter is being reserved for a discussion of tackle—the really few pieces of equipment a man needs to be happy on the stream. But we were passing through what I have termed, in another book, the "tacklemania" stage. It hit me hard, and for several years I had definite growing pains.

At the low end of the graph I acquired a little 7½-foot wand that weighed 2¼ ounces. With it I spent many pleasant hours on several streams, principally the East Branch of the Croton. One pleasant afternoon, just outside of the town of Brewster, I licked a tough 15-inch brown trout on the little stick after a long fight. It was netted by Jo, who soon afterward was to become my life-partner. She used this rod later on the Beaverkill, and today I still have it and occasionally use it for small trout in the brooks of Vermont. It is a pleasant plaything, but that is all. A fly-fisher's standby must be made of sturdier stuff.

In looking back over the half dozen or more years during which I fished metropolitan waters intensively, I like to consider them as time spent in a classroom. There I really learned to fish; but what is far more important, I was slowly absorbing impressions, which are, in the long run, the big things in life. Among these are an approach, at least, to an understanding of nature, and the friendship of men who loved and deeply appreciated the beauty and mystery of the open country and of the creatures that dwell therein.

Though some of these old companions are gone, their memories will always stay green. Laurie Mitchell, who afterward became Zane Grey's companion and fished all over the world, used to love the Westchester streams. He was a beautiful fly-caster, having been brought up on Nova Scotia waters. But he never cared particularly for the dry fly.

Ray Schrenkeisen, Laurie and I would often take week-end

trips to some stream where we would fish, loaf and shake off the tension of the city. Laurie invariably stuck to the wet fly and as often as not beat us badly, fishing the same water we covered with floaters. This is right in line with what I have always contended—that if a man is a really good angler, he will hold up anywhere, using any method.

Beginners often complain that they lack the opportunities which we of an older school possessed. In a measure, this is true. Thirty years ago waters were less accessible and game fish were more plentiful. Also, they were less sophisticated. But methods of angling were cruder and tackle had not reached its present state of refinement. Fish-cultural operations, too, were just nicely getting started. The planting of adult fish was unthought of not many years ago. So things are not as unbalanced as they may seem. It is true that there will be more fishermen, but that means more funds with which to work because of increased licenses.

In this age of rapid transportation there are no more frontiers. Soon remote wilderness lakes and streams will be little harder to reach than was the Oronoco of my boyhood. Wilderness fish will not long remain in doubt of man's intentions, and will speedily become shy and cagy.

It will go hard with us anglers—newcomers to the game and veterans alike—but we shall have as much fun as ever. And in the long run, we'll take fish, whether in Westchester or Labrador. Handicaps won't stop us.

A true angler will never be denied.

When the mountain tops are cloaked with mist wraiths the angler should be on the river. This scene is typical of the Catskills.

The Bountiful Beaverkill

FAR UP IN A LONELY VALLEY the Beaverkill springs from the rocky earth, a tiny brook starting in the shadow of Double Top Mountain. This wild and beautiful Catskill region, forested with conifers and hardwoods, is the haunt of deer, bear and wildcat; the abode of the great horned owl, the shy pileated woodpecker and the lordly eagle. The Beaverkill is nurtured in solitude, but when it reaches the broad valleys of pastoral country it can no longer keep its secrets. One of America's great trout rivers, it is discussed wherever fly fishermen gather.

A few miles southeast of Double Top another famous Catskill river rises. It is the Willowemoc, the Beaverkill's twin. Taking a southerly course around a mountain range, it flows in a big loop to join the Beaverkill at Roscoe. From the Forks, or Junction Pool, down anglers know the river as "the big water."

Double Top and its surrounding neighbor-mountains— Graham, Slide and Hemlock—might have been content to mother two such thrifty youngsters as the streams which develop into these noted rivers, and then have considered their duty done. But they were not. Geologists can undoubtedly explain the origin of two other important trout streams and a large branch of a third in this small area. Anglers, being less realistically inclined, consider it merely a happy coincidence.

One river is the Neversink, which rises in a notch between Hemlock and Slide Mountains. The other stream, the Esopus, heads on the north side of the same notch. It flows down another watershed and finally contributes to the New York City water system. A small tributary of the upper West Branch of the Neversink comes down off Double Top. The branch of a third river is Dry Brook (from the original name *Dri Bucken*, meaning three bridges), tributary to the East Branch of the Delaware at Arkville. This small stream also bubbles up from the rocks of the maternal Double Top.

Thus are born five of the great trout rivers of the East, each with its virtues and its devotees. And of them all, the most romantic is the Beaverkill.

Those who have wet a line in this famous river—and their number is vast—need not be told of the varying moods and character of the water. Like the prima donna she is, the Beaverkill is never stable. There are placid, easily wadable stretches, but these do not endure. They are merely pianissimo passages played by strings and wood-winds; the crash of brass will be encountered around the next bend.

Like a great symphony, the river does not reveal itself at once. It must be visited time and time again, its moods and temperament studied, before understanding and appreciation come. The transient fisherman may leave, after a short stay, swearing that it is the worst trout river on earth. Another and luckier angler, striking the water right, will declare it the finest stream in existence. Neither is correct; they are too green to form a sober opinion.

The man who is looking for a "soft thing" is earnestly advised to shun the Beaverkill—that is, the big water, below the Forks Pool. It is not a violet-strewn path. With a good head of water running—and sport will be indifferent otherwise—the current is strong and heavy. It takes a hardy individual to buck it day after day. The bottom, in most places, is vile. Rocks from the size of a grapefruit to that of a grand piano beset the path of the wading man. There are many deep holes and drop-offs into which an incautious wader may innocently step and find himself in trouble. And to top it off, the Beaverkill is noted for cross currents and a cut-up surface, which create drag and multiply the problems of the dry-fly angler. But there are also fish in numbers—or were up to a few years ago—and atmosphere of a quality to satisfy the most prosaic person.

From Roscoe downstream the pools are all named, and an angler familiar with the river will know what you are talking about if you tell him that you took a two-pound brownie in, say, Hendricksons. Here is a list of the pools in their order, as I recall them, together with brief notes on their characteristics. I expect to hear from old habitués of the river to the effect that I am mistaken, here and there, and that will be understandable, for circumstances have prevented my fishing the

Beaverkill for a decade. In the main, however, I think the list is fairly accurate. I am indebted to my old friend Walt Dette for helping to bolster a flagging memory.

The Forks or Junction Pool is formed by the confluence of the Beaverkill and Willowemoc in the town of Roscoe. It is famous. Every one who has visited the section has wet a line in it, and it has surrendered many a noble trout. It may be fished from several points, but my favorite spot was the stretch from the tail of the pool upstream on the railroad side. There is broken water here, with many good pockets where fish lie out and feed when there is a hatch on. The prize location was the head of the pool, to be reached just before dark. When they were really coming, you could depend upon hitting some good fish as long as you could see a fly float.

Ferdons is the next important pool downstream. It has pocket water at the head, with a long slick tail where good browns feed on a hatch. Usually unproductive during bright weather, Ferdons often proved a winner in the evening or on a gray day. It was easy to wade and to fish.

Quite the opposite in character is Hendricksons. I say "is" advisedly, for I feel quite confident that nothing short of an earthquake could change it. And, so far as I know, they haven't had any earthquakes up that way. Hendricksons has always had the reputation of being one of the meanest pools, not only on the Beaverkill, but on any river you want to name. It is strewn with huge boulders, some of them the size of a one-car garage, filled with deep holes and sunken ledges. Due to the narrowing of the river at that point, the current is strong and treacherous. It is no place for the timid man or the beginner. But if fished from the tail, or at a few points on the railroad side, it is well worth while.

Horse Run Pool is named from the small brook that trickles down from the mountain and enters the river at this point. It is a long rip of white water, with excellent pocket runs. This used to be a favorite spot for rainbows, which love fast water.

Cairns is one of the most popular and easily fished pools on the entire river. Located near the state road, it is handy and conveniently reached. The river is wide at this point, and from the shallow tail of Horse Run the bulk of the current swings along the O. & W. railroad embankment, entering Cairns pool as a gentle but strong riffle. The water deepens abruptly to eight or ten feet at normal level, and a long ledge extending a great distance affords excellent cover for trout.

Fishing from the roadside, you can wade out in gradually deepening water to within comfortable casting distance of the far bank. The bottom is gravelly and easy to wade. The biggest objection to Cairns Pool was its popularity. It was hard to find a time when there weren't from three to six rods planted strategically and pretty permanently from the head of the pool to the tail.

Wagon Wheel Pool is considered by many to be the tail of Cairns. It was always a pleasant spot to fish, though not on a bright day. I can recall hooking several good brownies there late in the evening. It was reasonable water for the fisherman.

Schoolhouse Pool is reached by scrambling down a steep bank, just off the state road, and cutting through a strip of woods. It was always a good bet for those who wanted to take the trouble, especially during a hatch of flies.

Next comes Lockwoods, a long deep pool with a broken surface for about half its length. In the middle '20s this piece of water was famous for really big browns. I recall one year when, during the May-fly hatch, at least eight fish weighing four pounds or more each were taken from Lockwoods. They were all caught on the dry fly, most of them during the day. It was about mid-June, and water and weather conditions were ideal.

The pool is well situated, with a good bottom and easy casting conditions. The current is even and has very little tricky drag. Being perfect dry-fly water and the haunt of big trout, it is easy to understand why Lockwoods is as popular as a vivacious, red-haired girl at a picnic.

A strip of rather indifferent water is usually by-passed by anglers on their way downstream to the next fishing spot. This is Mountain Pool, conceded by everybody to be one of the real beauty spots of the Beaverkill. A gravelly beach with gently sloping bottom—ideal wading conditions—forms one shore. There is ample room for the back cast.

The opposite shore is almost theatrical in effect. Rising steeply from the shadowed water, a great ledge of rock looms over the river. It is heavily clothed with lichens, moss, oxalis and other woodland plants. Pine, hemlock and young hardwoods cling to the shallow top soil and ascend the slope to apparent infinity; the space they do not occupy is filled with an intricate network of laurel and rhododendron. Half a dozen varieties of ferns add accents of lighter green. Mountain Pool is beautiful at any time, but to see it at its best one should be there when the rhododendron is in bloom.

Strangely enough, this idyllic spot has not been, in my experience at least, a consistent or heavy producer. At times I have taken some good fish from it; on other occasions, when conditions seemed right too, it would let me down scandalously. One of the best rises of trout I ever observed there occurred on a day when I was making a water-color of the spot. I had left my tackle home, fearing just such a thing. It was exquisite torture!

Mountain Pool is noted for tricky currents, which create annoying drag, but Lower Mountain, a few hundred yards below, is a very satisfactory spot. There the bulk of the current flows along a deep ledge, and it is a great place to drift a floater. Every once in a while some one would take a whopping brownie out from under the ledge, and the water was usually good for several fish up to a pound. Unfortunately, too, it used to be infested with small black bass, which would take a dry fly much too enthusiastically—a most annoying thing when you were working hard for a rising trout. It was in Lower Mountain Pool that Pres Gardner caught the big smallmouth, the incident cited in the chapter, "River Bass."

Mention Painter Bend—the next pool downstream—and at once you think of an artist hard at work, with canvas and brushes, struggling with the problem of values, color and atmosphere. I thought so too when I first heard of the place, but it's not that. Painter Bend is picturesque enough, though not in a class with Mountain Pool, but the name comes from the old colloquialism for the cougar, or puma. This great cat has been traditionally known as the "painter" (panther) among old-timers. One of the tawny felines was reported to have been killed—or sighted—at this spot in the distant past; hence the name. It has been many years since a cougar roamed through any of the Eastern forest areas; so the legend must be very old. Whether it is true or not I cannot say. I hope so. It adds stature to an already fabulous place.

We are supposed to have a "painter" up around Randolph in Vermont. Many people have seen his track and heard him yowl in the dark of the moon. No one has seen him. I hope no one ever does. He might turn out to be a huge bobcat or even an overgrown tom of the roof-rabbit species, and that would spoil a peach of a story. Painter Bend is a little hard to reach unless you fish the stream, being on a loop of the river away from the road. It is a pleasant pool, and occasionally it proved productive.

We are getting far down the river now, as the next important fishing is at Cook's Falls. Here there is a good run and a pool, each named after the town. As might be expected, the water gets heavier and the stream wider—conditions which call for hard work in wading. Good honest steel-studded brogues are in order, and a wading staff is insurance against a nasty spill. The run has always been a favorite place for the dry-fly man who likes to fish pocket water. There, during the height of the hatch, many very large browns have been taken. The pool is good, too—or was—but because of its proximity to the village and the state road, it has been greatly overfished.

Cemetery and Barrel Pools, on down the river, have their adherents, though I never cared particularly for either of them. The former is overlooked by ranks of tombstones, and I found it difficult to concentrate on my cast when I thought of the old fly fishermen reposing under the sod and no longer able to hear the *blup* of a rising trout. It wasn't exactly fair to fish in such a place.

Chiloways, considerably below, is another beautiful spot, similar in character to Mountain Pool. A sheer rock ledge rises steeply up from one bank, and there is a good wading place along the other side of the stream. I have taken about as many bass from this pool as trout, especially late in the season. In fact, from Cook's Falls down to East Branch—where the Beaverkill empties into the East Branch of the Delaware—bass become a problem to the trout fishermen; bass and the ubiquitous fallfish, known as the chub.

Almost the last of the important pools is Baxters. There a long strip of water flowing close to the road affords about every type of fishing a man could want—pockets, slicks, pools, eddies and long glassy runs. There is much wadable water and, when a hatch is on, enough territory to keep an angler happy for most of a day.

In brief, then, this is a quick glance at the main Beaverkill —the famous big water—beloved of many anglers for generations. It is unposted, which means that it may be fished freely by any one so inclined. Though the sport has depreciated noticeably during the past decade, there are still many great

trout in its turbulent waters, besides smaller ones worthy of any angler's time and skill. They present a tempting challenge to one who loves to feel the press of the current against his legs and watch the golden flash of a feeding fish.

My introduction to the Beaverkill came in June, 1922, when I visited the stream with my old friend Doc Sweetser. We stayed at a farmhouse near Rockland, and on the first evening we took some twenty trout in a couple of hours' fishing.

It was a revelation to me, as I had not fished Catskill waters before. From that time on until 1934—a period of twelve years —I spent from two weeks to three months or more each year in the Beaverkill country, making headquarters at Roscoe.

Those who fished the river during that time will recall the remarkable sport to be had whenever conditions were favorable. They were truly years of bounty, a golden era during which the old stream reached great heights. Easy transportation has changed all of that; we shall never see the Beaverkill in her prime again, for in spite of the best efforts of the Conservation Commission fish will be caught faster than they can be planted.

Singing a dirge of regret never helped anyone. I do not, therefore, mourn the loss of what was, but, from the force of circumstances, can never be again. I am grateful for the memories I retain, as are the anglers who fished the Beaverkill in those days and caught not only trout but impressions and, best of all, friendship. Perhaps some of the men who waded the old river in the '20s and early '30s may come upon these lines. If so, they will recall their stream-mates, with whom they wet a line or swapped yarns in front of an open fire on a cool evening in late May or early June.

There was "Pop" Robbins, the dean of the Beaverkill, friend of every one—beginner or veteran. For half a century Pop paid court to what he always stoutly maintained was the grandest trout river on earth. Even when the old lady let him down, as she occasionally did, he was cheerful.

"Come a rain," he would say, "and you'll see. Why, gracious, it's only the middle of June, and we've got two or three fly hatches due yet. I expect the fishin' to hold up till the 4th of July."

Pop had seen it all. When he first fished the Beaverkill, the stream contained nothing but "native," or brook trout. The fish were small, but they were present in unbelievable numbers. Dry-fly fishing was unknown, and the practice was to work a cast of three wet flies downstream. The reception which the European, or brown trout, met when first introduced is well known to fly fishermen. The stranger was cordially hated. Anglers said that it was homely, lacked fight, wasn't fit to eat and drove out the native trout. The only concession they were willing to make was that the brownie did grow to a prodigious size.

Pop was one of the few who defended the immigrant almost from the first. He often told me that the brown trout was the salvation of the Beaverkill, and he quickly recognized the sagacity, fighting qualities and particularly the surface-feeding habits of a great game fish. The dry-fly method of fishing was needed to bring out the best traits of the brownie, and when it was taken up in this country Pop was one of the first to adopt it. Even during his latter days, when his eyesight had dimmed and his fingers had swollen with arthritis, he stuck to the floater, using a big fanwing or bivisible which could easily be seen. And he employed it with telling effect. Friends would make up casts for him in the evening, or he would hail someone along the stream and ask him to tie on a fly.

Pop had a deadly method of fishing a combination of wet and dry fly. One evening we were fishing in Cairns Pool, and there was a hatch of tiny midges on the water. Big trout were rolling and softly sucking them in, a short cast away. They would not pay the slightest attention to flies fished in the regular way. Pop asked me if I had any No. 16 Black Gnats. My fly box contained several; so he had me rig a couple of 4X leaders, tying a tiny Black Gnat on the tippet and a big, fluffy bisivible, attached to a short snell, about eighteen inches up the leader.

He laid a line out among the trout and let it drift naturally with the current. He told me to watch the bivisible. On one of the drifts I saw the big floater dart suddenly a couple of inches. Pop tightened up, and a 15-inch brownie broke out in full view, fast to the tiny midge. We took a number of fine trout that evening, and I learned a trick which has come in handy on many an occasion since. The dry fly merely acts as a bobber.

Having started his career as a wet-fly fisherman, Pop often used the method, especially at times when trout were not interested in floaters. He was an advocate of the "natural-drift" theory, and I can't recall seeing him impart movement to his fly. "Just keep in touch with your fly," he would say, "and if there's any current at all the fish will hook itself."

I spent many happy days fishing with Pop over a period of eight or ten years. We covered much country, from the lower end of the big river to the upper reaches of both the Beaverkill and the Willowemoc. His knowledge of the Catskill region was vast, and he had a wealth of lore which was both entertaining and instructive. Richard Robbins was a great angler and a fine gentleman; he was a man to know and to have as a friend. He passed on in January of 1937 and was buried in Riverview Cemetery, Roscoe, in a spot which overlooks the stream he loved so long.

Another colorful figure of the early '20s was Louis Rhead, artist and ardent fly fisherman. I spent some time with him on the Beaverkill during the season of 1923. He was then an old man—in years, but not in action. He possessed the enthusiasm of a kid of sixteen; he waded fast water sure-footedly and scrambled up a steep bank like a squirrel.

Louis Rhead had a great devotion to the natural-imitation theory, and he tied lifelike replicas of crawfish, hellgrammites, nymphs and adult flies. He would fish these diligently, day after day, and the empty creel with which he often returned never dampened his spirits. Anglers called him a luckless fisherman and kidded him unmercifully; but usually, when things were at their worst, he would show up with a brownie or rainbow of prodigious size and silently slay his critics. Louis Rhead was an idealist. He cast a beautiful line, gracefully and without effort. He got a great kick out of the river and all it stood for.

From 1923 on, the Beaverkill became increasingly popular, and it was fished each season by many of my Westchester

Brownie Somersaulting

County friends. Some of them who had been devotees of the Esopus for several seasons abandoned that stream and came over into the Beaverkill camp. Regular visitors were Ted Townsend, Lou Petry, Mel Rosch, Jack Krepps, Tom Foster and Ed Schirmer. Lou Petry traveled with a huge suitcase of fly-tying material and spent as much time in imitating trout-stream insects as he did in fishing. The demands of that gang were merciless, and Lou was just too good-natured to refuse anyone. I must confess to a certain amount of squeeze-play myself.

Early one June there was a huge hatch of the big yellow May-fly on the water. It was a year when the river was full of huge browns, and they were taking the natural with zest, but refusing all of what we considered "reasonable facsimiles." Lou took up the challenge. His reputation was at stake, and he worked long hours in an effort to tie the perfect Yellow May. One evening he handed me a beautiful example and told me to try it next day. It would have fooled another May-fly. Lou apologized for the hook; it was one of those infernal contraptions known as a barbless hook, with a kink just under the point. He had run out of straight hooks and had been forced to use it.

I met Ted Townsend at the upper end of Hendricksons on the following morning, and we settled down to some serious fishing. Big brown trout—some of them weighing three and four pounds—were rolling over in front of us. The fly hatch was as heavy as ever, and fish were on the feed. After trying several patterns without success, I thought of Lou Petry's masterpiece and tied it on. In order to get any rises, we had to use very fine leaders; so anything but a gentle strike was out of the question. The fish were breaking not over twenty feet from us, and long casts were unnecessary.

The fly sailed out over the water and settled gently just ahead of the place where a fish had been rising steadily. It floated six inches, then a huge maw engulfed it. I struck as hard as I dared, and immediately the broad dorsal and back of an old buster swirled violently. The big brown turned and headed downstream; the reel buzzed like a locust on a hot day as the line zipped out through the guides. Immediately below there was a heavy rip, and into this the trout headed.

"So long, Ted. I'll see you later," I yelled as I ran along the rocky shore, following the fish. But I had forgotten that damned barbless hook. The big brown lunged out of the water full length, and he seemed to be 30 inches long. Before he struck the water again the fly had popped out. I would rather fish with a bent pin than that type of hook!

Incidents of my Beaverkill days drift easily before me as I write, like the mist wraiths which float over the Catskills after a rain. There is a temptation to go on and on, but space is limited and the place for a story, anyhow, is around the firelight in the evening. Besides, my experiences are, with slight variations, yours, whether they happened on the Beaverkill or somewhere else. I cannot, however, resist setting down two episodes which have always tickled me. One concerns a large brown which I caught without planning; and the other, just about the shortest battle I ever had with a fish—through necessity.

The first incident happened one evening just before dark at Barnhart's Pool. This has always been one of my favorite spots, and I find that I have inadvertently left it out of the list of pools on the big river. It lies along the railroad tracks, on a bend of the river away from the road, between Ferdons and Hendricksons. A heavy rip runs along the embankment at the head of the pool, and farther along the water flattens out into a fine dry-fly stretch. The shore is rocky, and shallow water extends out for a considerable distance before you strike what we ordinarily consider "pay dirt."

I had walked down from Ferdons and was strolling along the shore idly, studying the water for rises. Stopping, I tied on a large fan-wing Royal Coachman, as it was getting dusk and I wanted something I could see. I whipped out fifteen feet of line and dropped the big fly at the very edge of the shore to see how it would float. There was a slight wake in the still pool, and the fly disappeared.

I struck without enthusiasm, thinking that a fallfish had taken the floater. But there was weight and plenty of it, as a heavy fish swam deliberately into the current and headed for deep water. I jumped in and played him. The fight lasted for several minutes, and I netted an 18-inch brownie that weighed just over two pounds! You never can tell where a good fish will be lying out. If I had taken two more steps, that trout would have scooted for deep water, leaving only a disappointing wake.

The other episode has to do with the concrete highway that was being constructed along the river, replacing the old and worn macadam road. Not having a car that year, I had hiked down the railroad tracks and fished several pools, ending up at Cairns in the evening. Traffic along the road under construction was a one-way proposition, as half of the bed was torn up for a distance of several miles. That meant a wait of fifteen to twenty minutes for cars moving in either direction. If you were headed for Roscoe, for example, and missed a turn, you would have to cool your heels for a long time.

I was dog-tired from a day's wading and hiking, but I couldn't resist laying a floater on a promising pocket as I waded across to reach the road. As so often happens when one is not particularly anxious, a fine brown trout took the fly and I was fast. He was a strong, active fish, capable of putting up a long fight. Scarcely had I set the hook when I heard a hail from the road—"Hi, Bill, hurry up if you want a ride back. The traffic is about to turn!"

It was Ray Holland and John Taintor Foote. They had been fishing below and happened to spot me. There was a situation! I wanted that fish, but I badly needed a ride back. So I decided to gamble. Leading the fish past me by prodding him pretty hard, I made a swipe with the net and scooped him up. It wouldn't have worked once in a hundred times, and is terrible technique.

I stumbled and slipped across rocks, scrambled up the bank and made the car to the accompaniment of a chorus of protesting auto horns, impatient at the delay. After some minutes of untangling yards of loose line, rod joints and meshes of landing net, I subdued the flopping trout and measured him. He was a 16-incher, and had every right to be swimming free in the river instead of taking a ride in that car!

Most of this chapter has been devoted to the big river, the main Beaverkill after its confluence with the Willowemoc. Every one who visits Roscoe fishes some of the pools which lie between that village and Cook's Falls, or East Branch. It is thrilling water and the home of the buster. But when I think of the Beaverkill as an idyllic stream, the type of little river suited to the needs of what Father Walton termed the Contemplative Man, I turn at once to the smaller stream from Roscoe on up.

Flowing through a lovely valley, it is quiet, intimate and friendly. Though still very much a river, it lacks the gruffness and bluster of the big water. It is filled with clear, rocky pools and shadowy glens. Great masses of fern-brake festoon the banks, and mint beds growing out of cool springs, which trickle down from the mountains, add charm which is lacking on the larger stream. Most of the water is easily fishable, but the stranger must know where he is going, for the major part of the small river is posted. A number of clubs control the bulk of the good fishing, though there are several stretches open to the public.

A favorite spot with many of us who stayed at Roscoe was the lower end of the river, from the old iron bridge up to the first club posting, a short distance below Rockland. There were some fine pools and pocket water on this piece, and many of my best memories derive from it.

About a half mile above the village there was a long and very shallow pool which yielded mightily if you knew the secret. During bright weather you could see every rock and pebble, as the depth was scarcely over a foot anywhere, except at the head, where there was a small but deep pool and a sunken ledge. A stranger to the place wouldn't give it a second glance, considering it barren territory. But when the evening hatch was on, the water fairly boiled with trout—and good ones, too.

A friend from Connecticut visited me one spring, and I took him to this spot late in the afternoon. It was a brilliant sunny day, and the water was like crystal. As usual, the pool appeared to be utterly without prospects. Not a fin could be spotted anywhere, and my friend sniffed. "Too shallow," he said. "Reminds me of the mud flats on the Sound when the tide is out."

We returned when the sun had sunk behind the mountain and dusk was settling down. I told him to wade in cautiously and plant himself in a certain spot. The water was not over six inches deep, and the situation certainly seemed implausible.

In a few minutes I saw a very soft rise, pointed it out to him and told him to cast. He dropped a floater over the spot, and it was taken. A pound brownie came bouncing out and tore across the water like a streak. My incredulous friend had a hard time swallowing that one. We took a number of fine fish that evening, the "mud flats" backing me up beautifully. Trout often cruise around in very shallow water in the evening; this is a good point to remember.

There was a nice stretch of open water at Beaverkill Post Office, from the covered bridge down, another smaller strip at Lew Beach, and spots here and there on up to Turnwood. The stream gets progressively smaller as you go up, of course, but good-sized fish are often taken in spite of it. From about Craigeclare up we used to catch a good proportion of brook trout. A 10-inch fish would be large, and the biggest native I recall taking in the Beaverkill country was a 14-inch female, caught just above the iron bridge in Roscoe, on the small stream.

The cream of the fishing on the Beaverkill usually occurs from about the middle of May until the third week in June. Before that time the water is high and the weather is generally cold and unsettled. After mid-June the stream drops rapidly and the water warms up. Most of the insect hatches are over, and trout retire to deep pools. They lay up during the day and feed principally at night. If you don't mind missing a little sleep once in a while and enjoy high adventure, you can find it on any dark night in July or August.

While I wouldn't recommend these nocturnal forays as a usual thing—they are too upsetting—I would suggest that the uninitiated try at least one. There is always a chance of getting soaked, bruised or maimed in a minor way, together with the added attraction of hooking into one lollapaloosa of an old brown. Together with companions I have fiddled away many a pleasant night, when I should have been abed, as far down the river as Chiloways. Usually one or another of us would have some luck, but the proportion of big fish hooked and lost is impressive. Night-fishing is not good for a fellow; it leads to exaggeration.

Before dismissing the subject a few words concerning methods might be useful to those who have not been abroad on the river after dark. The weapon should be a good stout fly rod, something possessing gumption and spunk. We found a single, rather large wet fly or small streamer most effective. Sometimes we would tie in a dropper, number 6 or 8, a foot and a half from the tail fly. Invariably, dark patterns would take fish where others failed. My pet fly was one which I dubbed the "Higgins Special." It was a number 6 White Miller that I soaked for an hour in waterproof India ink. The treatment had to be repeated periodically, as the ink wore off.

The best technique is the drift method; cast across and slightly upstream, allowing the fly to swing with the current. Do not impart motion, but, as Pop Robbins used to say, "keep in touch with your fly." When a trout strikes you will know it. Usually it's a slashing yank which causes you to jump a foot. Trout generally hook themselves—or miss entirely. A fish hooked at night presents unique problems. You can't see him and don't know where he is; wading is uncertain and sometimes treacherous; it is impossible to keep track of snags, rocks and other obstructions. Like hazards on a golf course all of these things add to the difficulty of a sport which most of us feel already contains enough handicaps! A flash light is indispensable, but it should be used sparingly. Indiscriminate flashing will inform the enemy of your position.

Finally, look up your fish laws before sallying forth. Some states prohibit night fishing entirely; others limit the hours. It would be most embarrassing if you had to make up a little speech starting with something like: "Well you see, Warden, I just . . ."

In writing a chapter on the Beaverkill I feel like a man trying to paint a barn with a water-color brush; there is too much territory to cover for the materials at hand. A book should be written on the old river, and I hope that some day it will be done. There are anglers who have known and loved her for decades, who know her nature intimately. Their impressions and thoughts should be recorded before they pass on. The Beaverkill is one stream that deserves to live forever—regardless of what may happen in the future.

Though not in a class with its sea-run relative, the land-locked salmon is capable of putting up a good scrap when taken on light tackle.

The Tools of the Trade

SCIENTISTS TELL US THAT MAN has been on this old earth for a long time. At first he was a pretty elemental creature, interested only in getting along from day to day. His progress took a long time, but you really can't blame him for getting off to a slow start, for he had a lot to contend with. Such things as saber-toothed tigers and fierce prehistoric wolves, advancing glaciers and violent storms would stop us, too, if we had no means to combat them.

Ab, the cave man, had to string along somehow until glimmerings of intellect filtered into his skull and enabled him to devise means of beating the game and surviving. That he did a pretty creditable job of it is evidenced by the fact that we are alive today.

Ever since those dim days of long ago when man first started inventing things, his primary thought has been to make the product useful. He wanted something with which to cut down trees; so he fiddled around with combinations of sharpened stone and wood and made himself a crude ax. Later on he found that bronze worked better, and finally that iron—or treated iron, which is steel—was best of all. Though he had made a perfectly efficient tool, it lacked something. It was homely and clumsy. And since it is not in man's nature to put up with ungraceful objects, the secondary consideration of looks entered into the picture at an early period.

Cro-magnon man began designing some twenty thousand years ago, when he made a series of bang-up paintings on the walls of caves in southern France and Spain. That was in the realm of fine arts, of course, but the utilitarian angle was not neglected, as witness some of the fine furniture found in the tombs of the Pharaohs. It hasn't been a story of steady progress, of course; we have had sour periods, producing such quaint oddities as mission furniture and gingerbread trimmings on houses. But, in the main, we have steered a rather straight course.

On the long list of things that people use I have always felt that there are three outstanding examples of perfect harmony between utility and beauty. They are the violin, the double shotgun and the fly rod.

From a welter of principles, three men, at various periods of history, took what they wanted and created designs and ideas which are in basic use today. Stradivarius built so well that the very instruments made with his own hands have never been equaled in modern times. Only his contemporaries, Guarnerius and Amati, were his peers.

Though we have improved lock mechanisms and barrels, put the hammers inside and subtracted a superfluous trigger on the modern double shotgun, we still lean on Joseph Manton for beautiful design. He conceived the idea of the racy, straight-grip smoothbore—the most beautiful gun in the world.

And finally, for what concerns us most as anglers, we owe a debt of gratitude to Hiram L. Leonard for his life's work on the improvement of the fly rod. If you have ever attempted to use Grandpa's rod, you'll know what I mean. Ten-and-a-half or 11 feet long, it weighed around 8 ounces. It was made of Calcutta bamboo, with charred markings, had a grip of wound rattan, and was equipped with doweled ferrules. The line was fed through those inventions of the devil, ring-and-keeper guides, which continually jammed up a cast and created vast friction, thereby wearing off enamel at an extravagant rate. The action of the thing—if such it could be called—was never better described than by the term "willowy."

It took a powerful man to wield such a weapon all day long, and though Grandpa was that man he must have suspected vaguely that, somehow, there was room for improvement. There was, definitely, but it came slowly.

Those were the days of wet-fly fishing. Trout were plentiful, and the angler's needs were few. He made short casts—he couldn't make any other kind—fished leisurely and filled his creel regularly. Rod designs in those days were inherited from the English tradition, and until conditions began to change in this country it never occurred to anyone to improve tackle.

The big factor in the development of a really efficient fly rod undoubtedly was the introduction of the dry fly to America. The English had used the floater for a long time and knew the necessity of backbone in a rod, both to attain sufficient distance and to dry the fly by means of false casts. But English rods were long and heavy—frequently 11 feet, weighing 9 or 10 ounces. There was a reason for this: the fishing was done on clear, smooth chalk streams for large and extremely educated brown trout. Long casts were not only desirable, but necessary.

It is easy to see where such weapons would be useless on the turbulent rivers which are characteristic of most of our trout country. We needed something shorter and lighter, but still possessing that valuable attribute which our earlier rods had lacked—backbone.

How we arrived at efficient and beautiful fly rods in this country is a fascinating bit of history, in accord with our innumerable fine American accomplishments. There is no room for it here. Leonard is credited with many innovations and departures from tradition—the use of the infinitely superior Tonkin cane; the redesigning of ferrules, and the introduction of the rigid and eminently sensible snake guides. Whether he was responsible for all of this progress I do not know, but in time it arrived. He had many apprentices, and their names are famous in rod making to this day: Payne, Edwards, Thomas, Hawes. I knew Hawes and Edwards personally, and the latter built to my order one of the finest rods I ever owned.

Considered from the dual standpoints of utility and beauty, the modern hand-made fly rod has perhaps evolved about as far as is possible. Made of highest quality, selected Tonkin cane, split and joined with infinite pains, the progress of an individual rod, from raw material to finished product, is necessarily slow. There are fine nickel-silver serrated ferrules, which must also be made by hand, and a gracefully designed cork grip, which may include a reel-seat of the same material or butt up against a cedar seat. Snake guides are of finest tungsten steel, as is the top and first guide; no soft-wire stuff to wear into grooves and hack the finish off an expensive enamel line. Finally, the rod is simply wound, generally just at the guides and where the serrated ferrules meet the wood.

Unjointed, a fine fly rod is a lovely object to look at, like an article of well-made furniture. But on the stream it becomes a living thing, obeying the will of the angler, casting the line with the vitality which is in its very fiber, bending into a sturdy arc as it resists the onslaughts of the fighting trout.

Fine hand made fly rods are not cheap, but neither is anything that is really worth while. Forty, fifty, sixty or even seventy-five dollars—that may be the price of the rod you have your eye on. Outlandish, you may think. Really, it isn't at all.

Consider that you are buying something which has taken many long, weary hours of toil to make, plus years of experience and judgment. If the laborer is worthy of his hire, certainly the rod maker is cheating no one. He can produce only a limited number of rods a year, and he doesn't get rich doing it. If you are still hesitant, remember that you are really doing yourself a favor, for a fine hand-made fly rod will give many years of efficient service, outlast half a dozen cheap sticks, and never make you feel ashamed of it in any company.

Fly rods have always been a particular hobby of mine. I've played with them for years and have owned, at one time or another, quite an impressive lot—procession might be a better word, for they have a way of coming and going.

Friends sometimes ask me to help them select a rod. I always do it with hesitancy, because a rod is an individual thing with personality, and one that I took to might not suit my friend at all. If, after a short acquaintance, they failed to get along, I would feel like one who had unwittingly promoted a misfit partnership. And such people aren't popular.

Rods come in various weights and lengths, and there is a reasonable relationship between the two measurements. For example, a 9-foot rod generally weighs somewhere in the neighborhood of 5½ ounces. But the weight may vary from as little as 5 to as much as 6 ounces or more. Some of this may be ac-

counted for by hardware—a metal reel-seat, for example—but mostly it's in the wood. And the amount and quality of the bamboo are what give the rod its most important attribute—action.

It is readily apparent, of course, that a heavy rod will have a stiffer action than a lighter one of a given length. But we encounter a much more subtle problem in the case of two rods with identical dimensions—weight and length—having entirely different actions. How is this explained? Largely by the distribution of weight in the joints.

What then constitutes action?

It would take a bold man to make an arbitrary statement, for there are many considerations. The type of fishing one does, his build and physical resources, his temperament and inclinations—all of these enter into the case. While it is a common mistake to get a rod that is too whippy, it is also possible to lean over too far on the other side and get a mean, stiff stick that will knock out your wrist and forearm in a morning's casting.

The happy medium, as with everything else in life, lies somewhere in between. I can only refer to my own taste, and after many years of experimenting I'm not quite sure of that. Few anglers ever reach the point of complete satisfaction; they're always looking forward to something a little better.

At the present time I own three rods—this being one of my low spots—but the greatest part of my fishing is done with one of them. This is an old favorite of ten years' standing, and as straight and rugged as a Navajo Indian, though it has been through some keen campaigns with me in several parts of the country. It is a Thomas Brown Tone, 8½ feet long, weighing 4⅝ ounces. It is wrapped only at the guides and ferrules, which are gun-metal finish. The action is that known as "dry-fly," a vague expression at best. It is considerably above "soft," but far enough from "tournament" to be perfectly comfortable to the wrist and forearm during a long day's fishing on the stream.

This rod handles a D double-tapered line perfectly and is efficient at all ordinary and sensible fishing distances—15 to 50 feet. And that, incidentally, is where most of our trout are caught. When I want to "reach for one," a fish rising across the river seventy or eighty feet away, the rod will accommodate me; but I am not a distance caster, having neither the wrist for it nor the inclination.

With the 8½-footer I have whipped some big browns, rainbows and tough small-mouth bass in fast water. I have faith in it and feel that it won't let me down. The beginner, looking for an all-round rod, could do much worse than to choose one like it.

The second stick is another Thomas 8 feet long, weighing 3⅝ ounces. It has a medium action, a little softer than its big brother, but it is an extremely sweet rod to fish with, especially on small streams. Hook a pound fish in a pool where there is not much water, and there's fun ahead. Usually I fish this rod where trout run from 8 to 12 inches.

Finally, there is a pretty little plaything of 2¼ ounces, 7½ feet long. It seldom comes out of its case any more, though when I acquired it, over twenty years ago, I used it a lot on the Westchester streams. It is one of the original Cross rods, hand-made, and of such excellent material that it is good today.

Long ago I decided that it is desperately easy to go rod-crazy. They're such fascinating things that in no time at all you can sink a small fortune in a cabinet of them. You will probably end up by using one rod; so why not buy that one in the first place and be done with it?

For anything on the fly fisher's list up to Atlantic salmon an 8½-footer like the one described will do—at least on Eastern waters. That is my advice to the beginner; the old-timer, having been through it, isn't interested in what I might think, anyway. But whether I shall follow it is a question. Rods are such fascinating things, you know!

I have given much space to the fly rod because it is the most important part of the angler's equipment. What needs to be said about reels can be covered in a few words. This is by no means intended to be a technical discourse on the practical angle of tackle. There are many fine books on the market, written by experts—some of them my good friends—and they are filled with the knowledge that the newcomer seeks.

In brief, the fly reel performs one important function: it holds the line and keeps it out of a fellow's way while he manipulates it with his left hand in casting and much of the time while playing his fish. It is unlike the bait-casting reel, which feeds line directly off a revolving drum. This being true, it is apparent that the simpler a fly reel is the better.

It should be a narrow spool, single-action affair, of rugged construction with a fixed click. Years ago we used to think that the only fly reels fit for use came from England. They were beautifully machined things with a genuine agate-ring line guide, gun-metal finish and the name of a saint engraved on a silver plate. The cost was pretty close to a quarterly interest instalment on the mortgage—for one reel, I mean.

But now we know better. For it is possible to buy in this country as fine a fly reel as anyone needs for a fraction of the cost of the imported article. The reel should be of a size to fit the rod, but beyond that little more thought need be given it.

But the problem of a line, as every experienced angler knows, is not nearly as easily solved. The principle of fly-casting depends upon the relationship of rod to line. You have a flexible stick which feeds out line through guides. You give the stick a push through the air and the line follows the impulse; push again and feed out some more line; the line travels a little farther— and so on. How far and how well you can cast depends upon the ratio of the line's weight to the rod's strength.

This is an elemental explanation of the phenomenon of fly-casting; it's so simple that a child should understand it. Yet, in spite of all that has been written about it, there is still plenty of mismatched tackle in the land.

The commonest mistake is to select a line too light for the rod. In that case the angler suffers, for he cannot obtain the maximum effiiciency from his rod. And in anything like a wind he is virtually licked, for even a powerful split-bamboo can't drive an underweight line properly, given the best conditions. Though the fisherman is being cheated, he is not doing his rod any harm.

On the other hand, nothing can knock the life out of a rod faster than to "over-line" it. Continued use of a line too large in diameter will remove the spunk from the best split-bamboo made and soften it up like putty. It will lose its action, take a set and become worthless. Of the two mistakes, this is by far the worse.

How can you tell what diameter line to use on a rod of a given length and weight? You can't—absolutely—but you can come close enough to it for all practical purposes. A good rod maker will recommend a line to fit any rod he turns out. Even machine-made rods, those of better quality, usually carry a line-weight suggestion on the card accompanying them.

In brief, the lightest rods, those from 2½ to 4½ ounces, will handle comfortably and safely an F or E line, depending on their action. A size D line is indicated for a rod from 4½ to 6 ounces; over that weight, C, or light salmon, is in order. This information is, of course, very sketchy. Action is really the governing factor. I have seen 8-foot rods weighing slightly under 4 ounces handle a D line perfectly, while the same line would seriously strain a 9-foot, 5-ounce rod of soft action. Selecting a line is a matter of judgment, plus some experience. When uncertain, it is best to seek expert advice, rather than to take chances.

When I started fly-fishing, domestic enamel lines were

pretty ordinary products. Tapers were unheard of, and a soft-dressed line didn't exist. Not knowing any better, we were perfectly happy. We cast well enough and got along fine until some restless soul sent to England for one of those double-tapered, vacuum-dressed products. He showed it around, and after that it was just another Garden of Eden story. And the apples had their price too, because an imported line cost like the very mischief. Fifteen to eighteen or twenty dollars was the price of a Halford or a Hardy double-taper. Among the poorer gentry, of which I was one, there was a heap of grumbling.

The wails fell on attentive ears, for soon progressive American manufacturers began experimenting with the improvement of lines. Among these were the Crandalls of Ashaway, Rhode Island. Julian and his father had a creditable line, double-tapered and well in advance of the old level, hard-finished lines, as far back as 1923. I fished one of these and found it good. Since then, they and other manufacturers— Gladding, Newtown, U. S.—have been steadily going forward, until American lines are now as good as any made. With the introduction of nylon a few years ago, it is hard to see where there is room for improvement.

A few anglers, especially those who habitually fish a short line, still like a level line. But the majority of us prefer a taper, chiefly because of its greater delicacy. The ordinary double-taper starts at H and gradually increases its diameter for a distance of about 18 feet, where it assumes its full weight of E, D or C. The line is graduated at both ends; hence the term "double taper" and the designation "HDH." The advantage, of course, is to dispense with weight at the end and to put it where it belongs—back in the body of the line, where it will work for you after you have your cast started and are "laying into it."

For all practical fishing purposes, the ordinary double-tapered line is about perfect. The chap who yearns for distance may want a torpedo, or one of its variations. It is the line used principally at tournaments nowadays and undoubtedly has its advantages in the field of eating up space. But I do not consider it a particularly pleasant line for the stream for ordinary dry-fly work.

Tapered lines come in 30-, 35- and 40-yard lengths. For ordinary stream-fishing they are long enough. But it is well to splice on enough linen backing line so that the drum of the reel will be nearly filled. And if you ever fish for grilse, large browns or rainbows and need to feed line out to a running fish, you'll have it to feed.

A good line deserves the best of care. Don't walk on it; iron-studded brogues won't help the finish a bit. Don't scrape it over rocks or tree trunks, or leave it on the reel in the broiling sun for long periods. Use only the best of mineral-base greases and wipe off the excess. Don't use deer fat. It sounds romantic, but animal fats contain injurious acids which will gradually decompose the finish. And finally, never leave lines on reels during the off season. Coil them loosely in foot-long loops and hang where the air can strike them, in a closet; or use storage reels. Then you'll never have to worry about tacky fly lines.

Most of this chapter has been devoted to rods, reels and lines, because they are the basic and fairly permanent part of the fly fisher's gear. Leaders and flies are the expendables; they come and go like the whims of weather. Furthermore, they deteriorate with use at an alarming rate, so that a fellow can never be quite sure of his inventory from trip to trip. It is this transitory aspect of an angler's belongings that impoverishes him and keeps the tackle dealers fat.

Leaders, fortunately, need not impose a problem, provided the angler doesn't become too technical. There is such a thing as acquiring a gut gauge, list of standard diameters, probably even a slide rule, and figuring out perfection to the ten-thousandth of an inch. These lines are not addressed to gents of such leanings, who are far and away my mental superiors. The aim here is merely to suggest to the uninitiated what he needs to struggle along with during the course of a day's fishing and remain reasonably happy.

For all ordinary dry-fly fishing, tapered leaders 7½ to 9 feet in length will be sufficient. They should graduate to tippets of four sizes to cover a range of fish from small trout to landlocked salmon or grilse and varying weather and stream conditions. These weights should be, from the finest to the heaviest: 4X, 3X, 2X and 1X. Practically never will the dry-fly man need anything stouter than 1X, even for grilse weighing up to 8 pounds. The majority of his trout fishing will be done with leaders having 3X points. In bright water when trout are shy, 4X points will be effective; also for use with tiny flies.

Wet flies may be fished most effectively on dry-fly leaders with 2X points. Tie in a dropper 18 inches or two feet above the tail fly if you wish. Bucktails and streamers are handled perfectly on 1X points.

It is well to carry with you a few strands of leader material, in the form of loose tippets, in case you wish to lengthen your cast. There are occasions where a 10- or an 11-foot leader will fool cagey trout, but it's a hard job to fish a leader much longer than the rod, especially in a wind.

Concerning material, much could be said, but most of it would be totally unnecessary. Only a few years ago we had but one possible choice—natural silkworm gut. Then, with what seemed like a rush, we were handed the modern miracle of nylon. Old-timers are conservative, and changes do not come easy to them. But a reasonable amount of familiarity with anything will break down prejudices. There is no doubt but that nylon, a synthetic product, has definite advantages. It does not deteriorate as fast as gut and is a much more flexible product. It's biggest advantage is the fact that it can be tied dry, thereby forever eliminating the nuisance of the leader box.

I usually carry both nylon and natural silkworm gut leaders with me. But only the finest quality of the latter will do. There is no abomination like a cheap gut leader, with its flat places, ungainly knots and general lack of efficiency. Leaders are pretty much a matter of personal taste, and every angler, sooner or later, works out the problem to his own satisfaction.

To a fly fisherman, no subject is quite as fascinating as that branch of his sport which deals with lures—the beautiful, feathery counterparts of aquatic insects which are the very basis of his art. He will buy them, fish with them, fondle them, invent new patterns—in short, become so absorbed that time ceases to exist. It's a good deal like Dave Newell's commentary on conversation. He complains about the hurry and bustle of New York—and heaven knows, I agree—where people have no time for pleasant talk.

"Now, in Florida," Dave says, "we like to sit around and chat. Why, I'll talk for five minutes, five hours, or five days when I meet up with somebody I like."

Knowing full well the infinite possibilities of the subject and the limitations of this work, I am forced to exercise a restraint which I know will be hard. For I dearly love to talk flies.

The art of fly-tying has advanced greatly during the past twenty-five years, and the credit is due largely to anglers who, experimenting with eager enthusiasm, have changed the conception of patterns to apply to our waters in various parts of the country. Many of the old standards are still effective, and probably always will be. Among these are flies which I used in my boyhood—Cahill, March Brown, Stone Fly, Hare's Ear, Royal Coachman, McGinty, Brown Palmer, Professor, Gray Drake. They are fish-takers, under the proper conditions, tied both wet and dry.

But patterns of comparatively recent origin, practically replacing most of the old-timers, have become the standards of today. In the main, they are "buggier"-looking and, especially when tied as floaters, are probably more effective. Every angler has his own favorites.

A partial list of the flies I try to keep in my boxes reads something like this: Quill Gordon, Light Hendrickson, Gray Fox, Red Fox, Light Cahill, Spent Woodruff, Spiders (brown, black, gray), Bivisibles (blue, brown) and Pink Lady, Petry's Orange Eggsac and Lemon Woodduck. That, of course, just scratches the surface. But I feel that, with the addition of one absolutely indispensable fly, I could get along almost anywhere. That pattern is the fan-wing Royal Coachman, the old wheel-horse without which few dry-fly anglers could long be happy.

In the field of wet-fly fishing, vast improvements in lures have been made, and each season marks the birth of more patterns. Some die out, but others live on to take their places among the immortals. Included in any list of sunken lures would be such killers as these streamers and bucktails, all of compartively recent birth: Mickey Finn; the various Optics, or eyed bucktails; Green, Gray and Black Ghosts; Marabous; Polar Bear and dozens of variations of the bucktail.

Patterns are legion, and if, after acquiring several gross of flies, an angler feels frustrated he still has recourse to a professional fly-tyer, who will carry out individual whims to the letter. The Dettes of Roscoe, New York—Walt and Winnie—who are among this country's top tyers, make up many special patterns each season at the request of anglers. Not many of the designs live long, but they please their sponsors.

This brief resume should be enough to give the beginner an idea of the infinite length to which the thing can be carried if it is not stopped in time. The most sensible advice I can offer is to acquire a modest basic collection of standard patterns to serve as a nucleus. Three or four dozen will do to start with, and they will prove useful almost anywhere. Then, when visiting different waters, find out what fish are taking and buy flies locally—and buy sparingly.

For dry-fly fishing, purchase flies tied on Nos. 10, 12 and 14 hooks, with a few No. 16 for clear, low-water conditions. Model Perfect, Sproat or Hall's turned-up eye hooks are all good for floaters. Look for flies tied with stiff cockerel hackle, and don't go in for heavily dressed, fluffy affairs. They look pretty in the showcase, but are clumsy, both in the air and on the water.

Wet flies should always be on the lean side, sparsely hackled and with thin wings. A heavy sproat or Limerick hook helps greatly to sink the fly fast and let it travel in mid-water, where a properly fished wet fly belongs. Clipping about half the dressing off an overly plump commercial fly will give it an unexpected potency. In fact, I often prefer a bedraggled, trout-chewed fly to one fresh from the shop; it seems buggier.

Aluminum fly boxes, with compartments for drys and clips for wets, are my choice, though plastic containers have much in their favor. Tweezers, a small scissors, oil bottle, line grease and blotters are all a part of the fly fisher's equipment. They go into the pockets of a well-designed vest, which is an indispensable item—when genuine comfort is taken into consideration.

The creel should be of the long, narrow type and adequate in size. One that will take a 15-inch trout without folding gives you a sense of confidence.

A simple wide-meshed landing net with rigid and light wooden frame, suspended on the vest with a foolproof snap, is eminently sensible. Shun those elastic-cord contraptions. They are always getting caught and springing back at you like a rattler. You are apt to get killed or maimed.

In brief, then, these are the tools of the trade. Like the artist's brushes, paint and canvas, they are the means of building the picture—but only the means. Get the best you can, then forget them.

The object of your quest is, after all, a brawling stream, the song of a white-throat drifting sweetly on the spring air, freshly caught trout on a bed of ferns in the creel.

This is the thrilling moment for the dry-fly angler. The rise is more fun than the fight—especially when the trout is a husky, speckled "native".

New England Chips

FROM THE ANGLER'S STANDPOINT, the possibilities of New England are truly impressive. Within the borders of any of the six states a man who feels the urge to wade a stream can find an opportunity to express himself. Even tiny Rhode Island has some charming little rivers inhabited by the dashing trout. It is quiet fishing, for the most part, in a delightful, pastoral country. On the other end of the scale the angler may have Maine, with its vastness and its infinite variations. He may have it literally, too, for nowhere in this land is a person made to feel at home more completely and quickly.

We have been favored, geographically, with the bounty of nature. She has thrown up the great Appalachian range and watered its length with a far-spreading network of flowages which start as springs and tiny brooks and end in the sea as mighty rivers. This is the playground of armies of city-ridden people who love to feel the spring of a split-bamboo rod and hear the soft plop of a rising fish. It services their desire and needs. Within the space of an overnight's train ride they can

81

reach the farthermost limit of this wonderful country and be, for a time, in another world. We should never forget how lucky we are.

New England is often thought of as a tradition, and this is right. It has a distinctive flavor which exactly fits the character of its people and the ruggedness of its soil. But it also has physical boundaries, and these start, at the southern end, less than an hour's ride from Grand Central Terminal in New York City. It would be logical to assume that the Yankee atmosphere had been completely obliterated long ago by the influence of metropolitan life. But such, fortunately, is not the case.

We discovered this fifteen years ago when we first moved to southern Connecticut to live "a few months." The months stretched out into years, and we have lived continuously in New England—later moving to Vermont—ever since. We intend to stay there.

Except in a few remote wilderness regions, fishing exists only by virtue of the work of hatcheries, operated by federal and state conservation commissions. Native wild fish began to decline in numbers as automobiles and roads increased. Left to itself, the situation would rapidly have reached a point where the only remaining trout would have been mounted specimens in museums. In fact, some pessimistic soul predicted that that was exactly what would happen.

But fish culturists have made great strides, not only in raising fry and adult fish, but in studying and analyzing waters. They investigate the chemical content, make a survey of aquatic vegetation, determine the state of plankton—the minute animal life present to some extent in all waters—and then sit down and prescribe. The aquatic biologist is to fishing waters what the doctor is to us. When a lake or stream isn't functioning, he will administer the proper medicine.

By this magical therapy miracles are being wrought. Often a valueless body of water is transformed into—excuse the trite term—a "fisherman's paradise," as was Sabbathday Lake in Maine. It once contained only pickerel, suckers and bullheads; now it yields trout of fabulous size and in quantities sufficient to attract anglers from far places. Sabbathday Lake was analyzed by experts, poisoned to rid it of undesirable fish, then built up by introducing food fish upon which game fish live.

The experiment attracted the attention of conservationists throughout the country. If so much attention is paid to one body of water in the state of Maine, which is rich in natural resources, it is obvious that sections not so favored can benefit vastly by intelligent work. Connecticut is a noteworthy example.

In 1920, I first fished in the Nutmeg State. A friend invited me to his farm near New Preston for a week-end trip, to wet a fly in the Shepaug River. It was early in May, and the weather was still cold. He warned me that the dry fly was considered ineffectual on the stream, even later in the season; that a wet Royal Coachman for dropper, with a Black Gnat or Brown Hackle as tail fly, would kill 'em. But you had to fish them fast—practically skip the flies over the surface.

Being possessed of a skeptical nature, I disregarded his advice and went my way, floating pattern after pattern—flies which would take trout over on the Westchester streams—on every enticing pool and run that I could find. The morning passed, and I was fishless. At noon I met my friend. He had a smile and a dozen fine brookies, from nine inches to a foot in length. That evening my creel also held fish, but they didn't get there via the dry fly. It was another proof of the old saw, "When in Rome—"

The Shepaug River is the outlet of a lake, and the water warms up rapidly as the season advances. Originally it contained only brook trout, and by early June the fish would ascend tributaries to find the cool water they require. The river would then be dead. The introduction of the brown trout, especially in the lower reaches, has provided sport for a much longer period of time each year. As in the case of so many of our waters, the European fish has proved a blessing.

Both the brown trout and the rainbow can stand considerably higher temperatures than can be tolerated by the brook trout. Both are good fish, taking a fly well—particularly a dry fly—and having the desirable trait of leaping when hooked. Of the two, the brown trout usually works out better; he is a homeloving soul and will stay put about where you plant him. The rainbow usually develops itchy fins when mature, and longs for a taste of the sea. Give him an outlet, and he'll find it.

Brown trout and rainbows are at their best in larger waters, where they have ample food and range. The Housatonic River from New Milford north, along Route 7, is a splendid example of what intelligent planting and management can do. Though this now-famous stretch of river is hammered hard each season by droves of metropolitan anglers, it continues to yield good fish—some of them weighing three pounds or more. It is also the home of some fine river smallmouths, which will take a bucktail or a streamer in fast water with the verve and dash for which the species is noted.

The Farmington and Blackberry Rivers are two pleasant streams which, in comparatively recent years, have been tailored to fit the angler. Once indifferent waters, they now furnish sport and food to thousands who visit them. In the early '30s the plebian and rather drab Norwalk River, a short distance from New York City, was the subject of intensive planting. It was a few minutes' drive from the valley in which we lived, and I often slipped over there after a day's work to cast a fly for an hour or two in the evening. The fish were comparatively tame; but they were there, and once in a while a pound brownie or rainbow would hit and help to take my mind off the then-current depression.

The near-by Saugatuck and Aspetuck Rivers, small but picturesque streams, paid constant dividends. The trout were brookies, not large for the most part, but willing and scrappy. The Saugatuck flowed back of our house, and several dams at various points backed up considerable ponds. These were inhabited by sunfish, pickerel, bass and, as they say in Canada, "the odd trout." It was a perfect school for a small boy, and my young sons took to it with far more avidity than they displayed for classroom work. On one memorable day young Bill brought home a 12-inch brookie. He trailed clouds of glory in his wake for months thereafter.

By traveling over the ridge and following a disused road we could strike a charming wooded stream which was seldom fished. The trout were dark and fat, and once in a while a pounder would be creeled. These fish had been in the stream long enough to become "natives" and were far different—in coloration, eating and fighting qualities—from the freshly stocked hatchery trout. An artist friend of mine who is an enthusiastic trout fisherman hooked and landed a 2½-pound brook trout in this stream.

Once, while hunting woodcock in the fall, I stood on a bridge over a deep pool in the neighborhood of my friend's triumph. It was a brilliant day in October, and the water was very clear. Several small trout were plainly visible, and as I watched them a huge squaretail hove into sight. He swam slowly and majestically upstream, unaware that he was being watched by excited and incredulous eyes. There was fully a foot and a half of him, which would make him no less a fish than the one my friend caught. I went away thrilled with the thought that such a thing could happen within commuting distance of the city.

In 1936 we left Connecticut and moved to Vermont. That summer we bought a farm on a hill, overlooking a lovely valley. There is a brook in back of the house, one over in the next meadow, and another in the woodlot across the road. But these are merely decorative features, serving to enhance the place with their sparkling waters and merry voices. They contain no trout.

Below the house, and bordering the property for a long stretch, a sizable brook tumbles down over a rocky bed to empty into the White River, two miles away. It is large enough to permit of fly-fishing, provided one exercises reasonable care with the back cast. Despite the fact that it has the daylights wormed out of it from the beginning of the season till the end, it contains a good many trout. Some of these are busters, like the two-pound rainbow which Bill took out of a pool at the foot of the hill a couple of summers ago.

This brook is chiefly useful as a source of supply for table trout. It is a comforting thought to know that you can pick up a few fish for supper and have the fun of taking them on a three-ounce rod. But its chief value is to "sell" Vermont to skeptical souls who have to be shown. If they don't go overboard because of the view from the front porch—and most everyone does—then I take them for a stroll along the brook. Late in the afternoon, when the sun's rays slant just right, I lead them casually to such a spot as the Rock Pool and pause disinterestedly. In about twenty seconds they are pretty apt to spot a rainbow fanning water nonchalantly, a rainbow such as might have served for a model of a four-color illustration in the prospectus of any of our better fishing resorts. Maybe there are two or three others with him.

"Good gosh a'mighty!" the visitor gasps in astonishment "Look at the fish!"

"Where?" I inquire innocently.

"Why, right in front of you, down on the bottom of the pool. I'll bet that big fellow weighs three pounds! Don't you know anything about these trout? Don't you ever—"

"Oh, *them,*" I reply, trying to keep a straight face. "Sure, brook's full of 'em. Let's go up to the house and shake up a little something."

That comes pretty close to the truth. Big trout can be seen at many points along the brook, and someone is always having a tragic experience—hooking one and getting cleaned out. It has happened to me many times, and some of my friends have

wept bitter tears. After midsummer, when the water warms up in the White River, big rainbows often strike the cool current of the brook and cruise up the stream. You are apt to tie into one of them when you least expect it; but holding him in limited water and with a light rod is something else again.

The brook-in-front-of-the-house proves of double value; it breaks down the morale of the doubter, and it is a tough testing-ground for those who think they can fish. Right at the head of the list I place myself!

Another enigmatical stream is the White River itself. Visiting anglers, seeing it for the first time, might classify it as a perfect trout stream. They should not be hasty; it isn't. The White apparently has everything—deep pools, long glassy runs, brawling riffles, stretches of fast white water and plenty of cover. It has beauty, and it has fish. But it also has temperament—a devilish amount of it—and it is very jealous of its fish.

On the White there is no such thing as certainty. One day you hit them, and it may be a week before it happens again. A small wet fly, deeply sunk and drifted naturally with the current, will sometimes take trout. Again, on a cloudy day, especially when there is a light drizzle in the air, you may tie into rainbows by using bucktails or streamers. They are apt to be fish weighing from two to four pounds or more. The trout of the White have nothing but disdain for the dry fly. Small fish will sometimes oblige you by rising, but I can't recall taking anything over twelve inches on a floater.

By going up to Gaysville or to Rochester, where the stream

is small, fair sport may be had both on wet and dry fly; but fish will not be large. After the first of July the White yields fair fishing for smallmouths. And occasionally an angler ties into a big old brown trout while working a bucktail through a pool in the lower reaches of the stream.

On the Pompanoosuc (or Ompompanoosuc) the story is about the same. There are, in fact, dozens of rivers like these in both Vermont and New Hampshire. The explanation is that they are "scoured" streams. Flowing through precipitous country, they receive the drainage from steep slopes all along their courses. After every heavy rain the streams tear and grind along, well over their banks. Vegetation is washed away, and the necessary plankton has no chance to develop. In order to maintain large fish in such waters, the conservation commissions must keep putting them in.

Fortunately, not all streams in the Twin States are of this type; if they were, we fly fishermen would be hard put to find sport on anything but ponds. Both Vermont and New Hampshire have good streams where a man can be reasonably certain of finding a day's fishing almost any time. The Battenkill in southwestern Vermont and the Ammonoosuc in New Hampshire should be rated along with the important trout rivers of the East. They are natural breeding streams for trout and have the type of water that makes good honest fish flesh, and makes it fast. Rainbows and browns weighing three and four pounds each are not news and do not crash the headlines. Furthermore, they may be taken on the dry fly. This also is

Fishing the Evening Hatch

true of the upper Connecticut River in New Hampshire.

Fundamentally, the fly-rod man is a stream fisherman, and this book concerns stream fishing. But who can resist the appeal of a pond or lake filled with native brook trout, just itching to take a fly? Vermont is especially blessed with many such spots, and I have had fine sport on some of them. The larger fish are most often taken on a deeply sunk wet fly, fished slowly with little twitches. Pond trout are usually thrifty. They are fat and deep in proportion to their length. And some of the most beautiful brook trout to be found anywhere come from ponds or lakes. Often the flesh is pink or red and above average on the table.

Chips from my Maine log are meager, for I have only recently started to hew. But I found the work exceedingly pleasant. An old friend once told me that he had hunted and fished in every state in the union save one—Maine—that he had heard a lot about Maine, and he intended to save it so that he would have something to look forward to. Years later he told me that he was not disappointed.

No Eastern State has been favored with quite the natural resources, from an outdoorsman's standpoint, as those possessed by Maine. She has ponds a quarter of a mile across and lakes thirty miles long: tiny brooks and mighty rivers; miles of seacoast; chains of lakes, connected by flowages, on which a man can travel by canoe for weeks on end. She has plains, hills, marshes and mountains. You can travel from sea-level to almost a mile up without leaving the state. And everywhere you will find something to do, whether you fish, hunt or just rest.

Perhaps you're tired and want a good rest, with a little mild fishing thrown in for amusement. The state is full of fine camps, made just for you. You will live in a comfortable cabin with a fireplace and bath, and eat at a central dining lodge. And how you will eat! When you feel like fishing, a friendly and skilful guide will take you out and show you where to catch squaretails (the Maine brook trout is always a square-tail), black bass or landlocked salmon. And you will take back something besides fish, too, for the Maine guide is noted for his homely philosophy and wit.

Maybe you long for something more rugged, a touch of the wilderness. You shall have it; just say the word. If you have a month to six weeks at your disposal, take the Allagash trip. Travel by canoe through an unspoiled country, fish till you're tired of it, camp out under the stars each night. You will see wild creatures of many kinds: deer, porcupines, perhaps a mink or otter and, if you are very lucky, even a moose or a bear. An eagle will soar high over a craggy peak, and fearless whisky-jacks—Canada jays—will attempt to steal food from your hand as you make noonday camp.

Maine is the original home of the landlocked salmon. Though these gamy fish have been planted in many places, as far away as Argentina and Chile, the species was first de-scribed from Sebago Lake, in the southwestern part of the state. *Salmo salar sebago* is a subspecies of the great salmon of the Atlantic, and it inherits some of the latter fish's fighting spirit. The landlocked salmon is found in a number of lakes in Maine, but where it occurs in streams and flowages it is of greatest interest to the fly fisherman. There it will take a streamer, bucktail or wet fly when conditions are right. Often, however, the landlock will prove as temperamental as any educated trout. Then only tiny flies, fished with great finesse, will fetch him.

Two other distinctions of the Pine Tree State are worth mentioning. It is the only territory in the United States where sea-run Atlantic salmon enter streams. And it grows the biggest squaretail trout in the eastern part of the Union. In the 1943 *Field & Stream* Annual Prize Fishing Contest third place went to a trout from Pierce Pond, Maine. The fish weighed a flat 8 pounds. That compares favorably with the famous Nipigon trout, fish that usually clean up the principal prizes in every contest. The angler who yearns to catch himself a real old he squaretail, something he can have mounted on a hardwood panel and hang in his den, can do so if he is willing to work a little. Trout don't really start to get big until they go over the five-pound mark in such lakes as Moosehead, Cupsuptic, Mooselookmeguntic, Caucomg— But here I find myself in deep water; a fellow is supposed only to fish these places, not spell and pronounce 'em!

It is impossible to fish, hunt or just loaf long in this country without realizing that Maine is something more than a state— it is an idea. Everyone, from the millworker to the banker, is interested in sport and in conservation. They know that they have something away above ordinary, and they mean to keep it, not for themselves alone, but to share with the thousands who visit them each year.

Having been favored so lavishly by nature, one might think that there is nothing to do but sit back and collect dividends. But the State-of-Mainer knows better. He realizes that you never get something for nothing, and that to maintain a thing you have to work; to improve it, you have to work even harder.

Last September, Dave Newell and I made a trip to the Rangeley district to try the fall fishing and make a short movie. We spent most of our time on the Kennebago Stream, one of the popular watercourses laid aside by the state as an experimental ground. Landlocked salmon were cruising upstream from the lake, and there were good squaretails in the pools. It was pleasant fishing, even though the salmon were in a most uncooperative mood. They boiled constantly in front of us, but refused most of our offerings.

Earle Doucette, our host, landed a 4½-pounder on a perfectly monstrous-looking fly which he drags out and fishes on any occasion when the cause seems entirely lost. He told me secretly that an old Indian medicine man put a blessing on it in exchange for a pinch of tea and a couple of dried cigarettes. I don't believe it. The salmon probably mistook the thing for a drowned bat and discovered his mistake too late.

Kennebago is a lovely stream, both to fish and to look at. It has some charming pools—Canoe, John's Pond, Cedar Stump—and when you hit it right you are apt to be kept pretty busy. The squaretails are an added inducement. While fishing in Canoe Pool a well-known guide and exhibition caster hooked a 3-pounder, played it up into shallow water and released it. In almost any place other than Maine such a trophy would have been rushed to the taxidermist and mounted!

And speaking of trout, we were taken to a pond twenty miles north where it was difficult not to catch fish. We kept count for a little while, and from the tabulation I named the place—One-a-Minute-Pond. You won't find it on the map, but there are many such spots up there. The fish were brilliant in their spawning colors and averaged from nine to eleven inches in length. We kept enough for breakfast.

As this is being written spring in just breaking in New York. The trees in Central Park are putting on their first flush of new green. The trout season has opened in Vermont, and soon we shall be going home—home to New England, where there are always chips worth gathering.

An angler who fishes silently and is observant may have the good luck to come upon a vain cock grouse strutting pompously before an utterly indifferent hen.

Streamside Distractions

AN OLD INDIAN LEGEND
is built around the theme that certain individual animals, birds
and fish have magical sources of protection during times of
danger. They are, therefore, free to pursue their lives upon this
earth until such time as old age overtakes them, and they pass
on serenely and undramatically. Anyone who has hunted or
fished long can almost accept this explanation; it seems to be
as good as any.

There is probably a huge old grouse in your favorite covert
which manages somehow to be on hand season after season,
in spite of wise dogs and good shots. Heaven only knows how
much chilled shot has whistled around him. The occasional
glimpses you get of him lead to the conviction that he was
hatched slightly after the Spanish-American War. He fills you
with admiration. After a while you get to the point where you
hope that no one will shoot him, though secretly you feel that
they can't.

Every country has its legendary buck, with rocking-chair
antlers, its huge old dog fox that is wiser than anything Aesop

97

ever dreamed up. And in 'most any stream there lives a trout that has, at one time or another smashed rods, lines, leaders and lures and finned back to his lair to chuckle about it. Anglers who have met up with such a fish will offer all sorts of explanations.

"Just as I was about to scoop him up, my foot slipped and I fell in"; "confounded branch floated over my leader and broke me off"; "hook was no good, and it snapped." These are all plausible reasons and probably true, but the interesting fact is that the trout still survives. After you've had consistent experiences like this you begin to grasp at the old Indian yarn, simply because you can't think of anything better.

One spring I located a big brown in a fern-draped eddy of the Beaverkill. It was an inconspicuous place and was probably passed unnoticed by dozens of fly fishermen each day. My introduction was quite accidental.

Wading across a gravel bar near shore, I saw a U-shaped strip of water which ran back from the main river for a considerable distance. The entrance was almost concealed by tag-alders and a growth of rank weeds. A small spring trickled down from some rocks at the extreme end of the pool. Ferns hung down so thickly that there was barely two feet of water from bank to bank.

Idly, I stripped line and dropped a dry fly at the foot of the spring. It was a cast of about twenty-five feet. The waters of the tiny pool bulged as though a tidal wave had struck them as a big brownie rolled up and smashed that little floater. He had a dorsal on him that looked to be three inches across. I struck instinctively—much too hard—and the 3X leader snapped like thread.

Wading up, I soon saw how such an apparently inconspicuous place could shelter an old dog like that trout. There was a pool of cold spring water at least three feet deep, and it extended a long way under the ledge.

That adventure was only the beginning. I stayed a week on that trip, and every day I visited the spot, casting my fly with hopeful anticipation. But always something went wrong. Once a puff of wind carried the fly to the bank, and I hooked a fern frond. For that mishap I was rewarded by seeing a shadowy form melt back into the rocky lair. Two or three times I felt that the trout was present, but not voting. I had switched to a 1X leader, with the hope of holding him; but, as so often happens, he must have seen it and refused to rise.

Hope ran high another day when the old trout rolled right over on the fly, exposing a spotted side six inches broad. But when I struck, there was nothing there at all. I might have known he was only kidding, because taking fish don't often act that way.

When the last day arrived, I determined to make a heroic effort; that brownie had got on my nerves. It was late afternoon, and there was a small hatch of gingers on. Approaching the pool cautiously, I stood motionless and studied the water in front of the ledge. A natural fly drifted over the ferns and dipped on the surface. Instantly there was a bulge, and I could almost hear jaws snapping together. The trout was still there!

I tied on a small Ginger Quill, but did not cast; I was much too excited. This was the last chance, and there was no sense in foozling it. In a few moments another natural came drifting across, and this time the brownie lunged out head-length. He looked enormous. Now was the time!

False-casting, I measured the stretch, got the fly traveling smoothly through the air, and let it settle on what I thought would be his nose. But an instant before it lit a brown blob rose up out of the water. At first I thought it was the trout, but no trout looked or acted like that. It swam down the current, leaving a wake like a canoe, then scrambled out on the bank, dragging a scaly tail.

Why that damned muskrat had to show up at that exact spot, just as I had the one real chance of connecting with the big brownie, is beyond me. After all, he had the whole river

to swim in, didn't he? Of course, I don't believe anything as silly as Indian legends, but . . .

An incident like that can annoy you when it happens; yet it doesn't take long to get over it. And it's good for a laugh long afterward. Look back over the years of your fishing career, and think of the many interesting and often amusing experiences you have had with birds, animals and other creatures that share the stream with you as you wade along and cast your fly. When you stop to analyze things, isn't this one of the big reasons why you go fishing?

A fly fisherman has a unique advantage in that he really is part of the landscape—or should be. Dressed in somber clothes, he is inconspicuous. He wades slowly, and as he casts his waving fly rod might well be a branch moving in the breeze. Wild things often permit a close approach, especially song birds. And a carefree fisherman can get a kick out of a phoebe, sitting on a branch a few feet away, jerking its tail spasmodically and scrutinizing the intruder with its shoe-button eye. That gay little bird is worth more than the most costly feathered inmate of the Bronx Zoo.

On any good day you will see something of interest—a long-geared great blue heron, patiently following his profession; a doe and a fawn, looking tawny against the deep green of hemlocks; perhaps a mother grouse, trying frantically to lead you away from her brood of chicks with the old broken-wing ruse. Or if you're lucky, you might spot a cock grouse strutting pompously before an utterly bored and indifferent hen. Swallows dip and glide over the surface of the water—they like aquatic insects as well as do trout—and a kingfisher comes clattering down the stream in noisy protest at your presence. These stream-mates of yours will enliven your day—and sometimes in a most unexpected manner. Here is an example:

On a fine June evening I was fishing a long slick at the tail of a rip on the Beaverkill. It was shortly after sunset, and there was an exceptionally heavy hatch of May-flies on the water and in the air. Trout were rising regularly all over the pool, and the mirror-like surface was dimpled with many rings. Vying with the feeding fish were dozens of swallows, skimming over the water and seizing the big succulent insects. Occasionally a bird would strike the surface, like a hawk making a stoop, and create a boil like a rising trout.

I was casting a Yellow May floater, an excellent imitation tied by my friend, Walt Dette, on a 3X tapered leader. The fly dropped about thirty feet upstream and had barely settled on the surface when a swallow dived down, seized it and soared upward—all in one movement. Before I could recover from my astonishment the bird was fifteen feet in the air and still hanging on.

I slacked off the loop of line in my left hand and yelled. Only then did the swallow discover its mistake and drop my artificial fly. Was he scared? Not at all! He circled the pool, flew by my head, not twenty feet away, and picked up another May-fly—this time the genuine article.

Another experience with a bird was equally strange, and

though it happened many years ago the details are vivid. I was fishing a riffle in the Pine River in Michigan with a wet fly. It was at dusk, and as I stood in shallow water, close to a sharply sloping high bank, I must have been inconspicuous.

The line was quartering downstream and swinging with the current. Just as I prepared to cast, with rod at a position of about 10 o'clock, forward, I felt a violent jerk. The rod was almost torn from my hand, and the reel screeched as several yards of line were ripped off.

It wasn't a trout; nothing which swam in the river would do that. Besides, trout don't fly several feet above the surface, wear wings and make a loud booming noise. My disturber of the peace filled that description and more. When he hit the line, he somersaulted a couple of times, nearly struck the water, recovered and limped away dizzily, disappearing in what must have been bewilderment around the bend.

It took me several minutes to figure out what he was—a nighthawk doing his usual evening beat down the river. Whether he had me accurately tagged I can't say, but that surprised, booming *whoosh!* of his, when he collided with my line, came pretty close to cussing.

At some time in his career every angler meets up with one of those woodland dramas which are constantly being enacted, though seldom witnessed by us. Wild creatures must prey upon each other in order to survive. They have no butcher shops in which to purchase lamb chops, chickens and steaks and so must fend for themselves.

As sportsmen, our sympathies naturally are extended to species in which we are particularly interested. We dislike seeing a kingfisher catch a fingerling trout, figuring with at least some logic that, if left unmolested, the trout might eventually grow up and benefit us.

Personally, I have never thought that the few kingfishers we see along a stream do a great deal of damage to our sport. Their principal diet is chubs, minnows and fallfish. And nowhere is there a more picturesque rascal than this frowzy-headed, sharp-billed bird. In the wild state he should be entitled to the few small trout he takes, if for no other reason than that his presence on the stream adds something to the angler's day. But around hatcheries or private ponds he must be controlled as carefully as are rats in a granary.

Trout have other enemies which are of no value to man, even in an aesthetic sense. Among them are snakes, which are positively repulsive to many people. Several varieties of reptiles are fanciers of fish as a constant item of diet. The worst offenders are, of course, the brown-mottled or almost black water snakes which one sees along almost every Northern stream. These reptiles, which are non-poisonous in spite of their rather venomous looks, are a constant menace to fish life and should be killed wherever found.

Other species of snakes, while feeding principally on warmblooded creatures, occasionally capture fish. Years ago, while fishing the White River in Michigan, I approached a pool around a bend to discover a mighty thrashing near shore in shallow water. Hurrying to the spot, I discovered a huge blue racer—a mid-Western phase of the black snake—with its tail and half of its body on the bank and the rest of it in the water, making a mighty attempt to haul in a trout.

A dead stick on the bank provided a convenient shillalah, and I brought it to bear where it would do the most good, across the serpent's back. Several blows partially paralyzed the brute, and I hauled him and his captive ashore. On dry land, another sock made the racer open its mouth, and the trout flopped free. Except for a mark on each side of the fish's belly, it seemed to be in good shape. When placed in the water, it swam off strongly. It was a brook trout about ten inches long. I promptly polished off the racer, a specimen fully six feet long, and felt righteous all day.

Another adventure on that same White River did not turn out so well because I, the observer, was unable to prevent a tragedy. Fishing a cast of wet flies on fine gut one late August afternoon, I approached a rather deep pool close against the bank. It was low water and so clear that the bottom could be seen plainly, as well as details of roots and branches which furnished cover. Every fly fisherman knows and loves a spot like that; it fairly shouts trout.

Moving silently to within fishing distance, I stood a moment, studying the current and planning a cast. A trout rose and took an insect off the water. That was before I had taken up the dry fly, but I had learned to drift a wet cautiously over such a spot, often with telling effect. An instant after the trout rose, and before I could cast, the whole run suddenly sprang into life. Trout in unsuspected numbers and all sizes began to race and mill around. They ranged from fingerlings to one of about a pound weight.

Mystified, I watched in fascination. Being rooted in the stream like a stump, I knew that they had not seen me. There was no predatory bird in the air. Where could the trouble lie?

In a flash the answer came. A long brown form shot out from under a concealing root and streaked through the pool with incredible swiftness. Quickly it seized a gleaming brook trout, turned in the water, made for shore, and climbed out dripping, with the twisting fish in its jaws. It paused momentarily on a root, and I recovered sufficiently to shout. That was a pretty surprised mink, but he hung on to his meal and slithered out of sight in the undergrowth in a twinkle.

Years later, I had another and amusing adventure with one of these sleek aquatic animals. It was the evening hour, and I stood knee-deep in the tail of a fine pool in the Beaverkill. There was a light hatch on, and trout were feeding half-heartedly, as they sometimes do at the beginning of a flight of trout-stream insects.

Casting steadily upstream with a dry fly, I had been rewarded with only a couple of short strikes. I had just laid out about forty feet of line to reach a boil where a trout had risen, and was taking in slack. The fly had floated back a few feet when, with startling suddenness, the water in front of the fly erupted. In the fading light I thought that an old brownie had smacked the floater and rolled over clumsily, as often happens.

Striking, I felt weight for an instant, then saw a mink flounder across the surface in mad haste and dive down out of sight. The fly popped back at me. What a surprise we both got! To get hooked by a fisherman's fly while hunting for a meal is something, it is safe to say, that happens to very few mink.

While on the subject of fantastic things that befall anglers I like to recall the time Ted Townsend hooked a woodchuck. It is not common knowledge, perhaps, but Brer Chuck is an excellent swimmer when in the mood. He will cross a stream if he thinks that the grass on the opposite side is a little more lush—just as he climbs a tree, either to feed on tender leaves or merely to get a change of scenery.

This 'chuck was swimming across a still stretch below Hendrickson's Pool down on the big river one afternoon, quietly minding his own business. Ted, who is full of the devil, spotted him and idly cast over him. The No. 10 hook caught in the hide of the chuck's neck. Both Ted and the grizzled swimmer were amazed. The latter lit out, and the former hung on—there was nothing else to do. It was a grand fight, lasting all of a half hour.

At last the chuck began to tire; then it suddenly occurred to the angler that the beast would have to be landed in order to be freed of the fly. The same thought probably struck the animal, too. He objected strenuously. It was an embarrassing situation.

Ted finally netted the beast, and hell broke loose. In imminent peril of losing a toe—for a mad woodchuck can bite viciously—he heaved the animal out on the bank and clapped a brogue over its back. The hook was worked loose, and the chuck waddled off, chattering and muttering imprecations. He probably had a sore neck for a few days. Ted lost a good net, had some of the backbone removed from a pet rod, but learned a valuable lesson which reads: Never mess around with wild animals when you are armed only with a fly rod!

Here and there we anglers have personal experiences with wild creatures like those described; but for the most part our role is that of observer. How much our contact with living things means is not fully appreciated until we stop to think about it.

Take away the flute-like voice of the thrush and the trill of the song sparrow; deny us that strange but delightful symphony of the swamp, the peeper chorus; remove the wheeling hawk from high above the meadow; strike out the panicky cottontail dashing suddenly from underfoot, the furtive whisking gray squirrel and hundreds of other wild things—and what have we left? The stream and the trout, it is true, but in such a lonesome world what real angler could long be content?

Animate nature is undoubtedly one of our big reasons for being abroad, equipped with the rig of a fisherman. We yearn to catch trout or bass, and with any luck at all we do. The birds and beasts go along with the activities of any day astream. They are taken more or less for granted. But there are other subtler things which intrude themselves delightfully upon our perceptions, rounding out our adventures to the full measure. All fishermen are aware of them, though perhaps not consciously so.

Wouldn't you miss, for example, the pungent tang of mint which you have crushed underfoot as you work along the bank in a woodsy spot? Or the smell of sweet-fern on a dry upland hillside? I can't resist pulling off a handful of leaves and sniffing them. And penny-royal has its distinctive aroma. It grows thriftily in some of our Vermont pastures, and it's always worth while to walk a few steps out of the way when fishing along the river to pluck a plant or two.

The river itself has a characteristic odor which is indescribable but nostalgic. It is a combination of moss, ferns, water-soaked logs and wet loam. One whiff sets an angler to tingling and hastens the process of stringing up the rod and tying a fly to the leader. I have often thought that this unique essence of the stream, if it could be bottled, would be a boon to anglers during the long winter nights when they are still months away from their sport.

Settle back in your chair, close your eyes, remove the cork and inhale deeply. Ah-h-h! The blizzard raging outside is transformed into white water racing over ledge rock. The trout leaps again, taking a May-fly in mid-air. For a few brief moments it is June and fishing time. Won't some sympathetic and inventive soul work on the idea?

Dozens of fascinating sensations add to a day on the stream. Certainly not the least of these are the trees, wild shrubs and flowering plants which the angler encounters along any well-appointed river or brook. Most fishermen are fair amateur naturalists, having developed the habit of observation. This knowledge is usually arrived at more or less subconsciously, curiosity prompting them to look up a bird or tree here and there. If they were willing to go a step further and spend a little time in study they would find that the rewards are rich and satisfying. There is a definite value in being able to tell a goldfinch from a yellow warbler and to distinguish the white from the grey birch at a glance.

On Northern waters during those traditionally chill opening days the pink-and-white blush of trailing arbutus, hidden among lichen-covered gray rock, reminds you that warm days are just ahead if you will only bear up. Wood violets, marsh-marigold, anemones, bloodroot, jack-in-the-pulpit, hepatica, trillium—the procession marches on, so that the angler who has time to look is never without accents of color. You can tell the time of year by the flora if you should ever be so fortunate as to lose yourself for a few months.

When the shadblow is on, it's May; golden-rod would mean late summer—and smallmouth time—New England asters and gentians herald the late season. You'll have to hurry, but there is still time for a few casts. Maybe it will be ouananiche, or a late run of salmon.

It's a whimsical thought, perhaps, but I claim that such a schedule—which it is easy to see is no schedule at all—would cure a lot of ills. Jitters, creeps, dyspepsia and nervous tension would just melt away. They can't last under the influence of such beneficence and serenity.

Summing up, that's what fishing is really for; it's the pleasantest and easiest care-killer known. And it has a powerful ally in all of these delightful things I have called streamside distractions.

The boss of the river is the smallmouth—a tough, hard-living, fast-fighting gent, worthy of every angler's utmost respect.

River Bass

THE FIRST BASS THAT CAME
into my possession left their native element suddenly and without compromise or previous warning. They were heaved high into the air, describing parabolas which placed them, gasping and flopping, many yards beyond any possible chance of escape. I was in my first decade, and wholly untrammeled by any hint of sophistication in angling.

If, when I was fishing for redeyes and crappies, a bass was foolish enough to bite, that was his own lookout. The sensible thing was to lean back on the bamboo pole and get him started skyward, meanwhile praying that hook and line would hold. Often the bass would come loose midway and land perilously close to the river's brink. The contest was brought to a quick conclusion by a sudden, headlong dive in the direction of the flopping quarry, ending, of course, with success for the boy or the bass. Half the time I won.

When one starts fishing very young, he invariably follows this practice. It is so hard to learn restraint, to play a fish cautiously and slowly and to wear him out by skill. It seems much

113

simpler to horse him out quickly and be done with it. Only by disastrous experience, repeated time after time, does the truth finally dawn. The memory of many an Indiana smallmouth, lost by the length of a hand at the water's edge, lives on and plagues me after forty years. Such is the make-up of an angler.

Nearly a decade passed beyond those early encounters with the river bass before I met him under circumstances which were happier both to fish and fisherman. An interlude of intensive trout fishing found me wading stream after stream, with no thought of anything finny save brooks, browns and rainbows. The fly rod for trout was the ultimate goal, and having reached it I wanted nothing else.

This blissful condition might have gone on for a long time had it not been for an old friend, Charley Justin, who invited me to fish with him for a day on the Flat River in Michigan. I used trout tackle—a 9-foot 5-ounce rod with rather soft action, 6-foot leaders and two wet flies. We waded and fished the riffles, runs and eddies much as one would work a trout stream.

The bass were plentiful and willing; furthermore, they were filled with a brand of spunk, vigor and pure cussedness which was an absolute revelation to me. A two-pound smallmouth would rip off fifteen yards of line, break out in a series of noisy leaps, and be across the pool, boring for the shelter of roots on the bank, before I realized what had happened. It was enough to shake the faith of the staunchest trout fisherman and make him wonder if, after all, his beloved speckled fish wasn't a rather mild-mannered and gentle creature.

After that first experience, mid-June and the opening of the bass season came to be a date to look forward to with eager anticipation. Besides the Flat River there were several other interesting and pleasant streams—the Thornapple, Cedar, parts of the Grand and the Rogue River, all of them productive of fighting smallmouths.

The best part of bass fishing was the interesting fact that the fish were less temperamental than trout and could be taken quite regularly at almost any time. Furthermore, the season extended right up until cold weather, the opening of the shooting season, leaving no awkward gap in the life of an ardent sportsman. These conditions hold true today, for the bass, though doubtless gaining some wisdom with the years, is too pugnacious ever to become a thorough sophisticate. I can offer no more sympathetic advice to the fly fisher who believes himself to be a trout purist than to try river bass just for one day. Something will happen to his former ideas, and it will be all to the good.

When I first started fly-fishing for the river bass, the sport was little known in our section. Fishermen took their smallmouths either by boat-fishing, skittering with a spinner and fish-belly bait on a linen line and cane pole, or by casting a heavy plug with a short, stiff rod. Catching an active bronzeback on fragile fly tackle was looked upon by the majority of river devotees as something just a bit too fussy. The more charitable of them thought it a waste of time. Considering that this was not long before World War I, we have certainly come a long way in our ideas of what constitutes sport.

Bass flies used to be simply enlarged versions of trout flies. You were advised by tackle clerks to purchase the biggest and gaudiest patterns on the shelf. Scarlet Ibis, Yellow Sally, Lord Baltimore, Parmacheene Belle, tied on No. 1/0 hooks, were numbers without which no thinking fisherman would venture forth. They were tied on double gut snells, and to be sure that no bass escaped the angler was solemnly advised to buy double gut leaders of a thickness sufficient to hold a 50-pound tarpon.

That such tackle scared away more bass than it ever lured there can be little doubt. We soon discovered that the drab patterns of trout flies—March Brown, Hare's Ear, Greenwell's Glory, Cahill—tied on No. 6 and even 8 hooks, and fished on a medium trout leader, were deadly.

Nowadays we have beautiful hair flies and bugs, streamers, bucktails, poppers and scores of other types of lures, besides new techniques for fishing them. We also have fine rods with actions suitable to efficient casting and at the same time easy enough on a man's wrist to make a day's sport a pleasure and not a penance.

I have always felt that the talents of the river bass extend just a little beyond those of his brother who dwells in the lake. It is true that they are both smallmouths—*Micropterous dolomieu*, if you are technically inclined—but the fish of running water takes on the character of its element. The wildness and strength of the current is in its fiber, and these things it transmits to the angler as it fights against the restraining fly rod.

The river bass is full of tricks, too; it leaps repeatedly and takes advantage of sharp ledge rock and sheltering roots. It will dash full tilt through a boiling rip, rub its nose on a gravel bar and continuously shake its head like a bulldog in an attempt to rub out the fly.

Does your bass seem to be conquered at last and ready for the net? Beware! A final surge and break may grant him freedom to fight another day. For the smallmouth is never licked until actually creeled.

In feeding habits the river bass is not unlike the trout. At times he will take on the surface, and then the dry-fly angler may have rare sport. Oftener, though, he is inclined to favor sunken lures—wet flies, bucktails, feather minnows or hair bugs—fished just underneath. In bright weather the best results usually are obtained by fishing a lure in mid-water. It should be cast upstream and slightly across, then allowed to sink and drift with the current on a slack line. When a bass strikes, there is never any doubt about it!

Many of our Eastern trout rivers contain bass. Usually they are small fish and are a positive annoyance, as they will often take a floating fly which is being carefully fished for trout. The Beaverkill from Cairns Pool downstream has too many small bass for the good of the trout fishing.

One beautiful June evening Pres Gardner and I were fishing in the lower, or second, Mountain Pool on the "big water" —which is to say the lower Beaverkill. There were few insects hatching, and the river was very dead. We had been casting steadily for nearly an hour and were, at the time, covering a long oily run alongside a fern-draped ledge by the shore, forty feet away.

Pres had on a Pink Lady Bivisible, usually a killer, but now apparently worthless. The fishing had degenerated into a sort of monotonous casting contest, and to break the boredom Pres sang out, "Watch this cast. I'm going to hook a good one this time!"

There wasn't any reason why that cast should have been any different from the fifty that preceded it. But the fly hadn't floated a yard when the water boiled. Pres snatched back, grinned and yelled, "Didn't I tell you?"

His rod doubled into a taut arc and the line sang through the water. Something about the way that fish tugged made me suspicious, even though he didn't break water and reveal him self; nor was he in any hurry to give ground. It was a grand fight, lasting for several minutes. At last I was able to net the fish, and my suspicions were confirmed. It was a small-mouth, about 16 inches long and one of the best bass I had seen taken from the Beaverkill up to that time.

"Yip-pee!" yelled Pres. "Didn't I tell you I'd have one to take home?"

"Sure," said I, rather sourly, at the same time reversing the net and dumping the bronzeback in, "only you can't take this baby home. It lacks two days till open season."

That was pretty hard to take; but, after all, we were fishing for trout. The bass would only be an unearned dividend.

Those who have not wet a line in the Delaware have a treat in store. There is much good water on the East Branch from Margaretville, or even above, down to the confluence with the main stream. But it is this river, the West Branch, which probably holds the greater interest for the fly fisherman. For one thing, it is bigger water, and the size of the average fish is in keeping. This is not to say that the angler is to look for anything phenomenal. In river fishing with fly-rod lures it is only the exceptional fish that will weigh three pounds. Most of them will run from a pound to two, but bass of that size have activity, vigor and speed enough to stir up the most jaded angling appetite. Six or eight such fish, taken during the course

of an afternoon's pleasant casting, are sufficient to make you purr like a cat full of warm milk.

If one likes boat-fishing, he can do no better than to take a float trip down the Delaware, starting at, say, Hancock and drifting by easy stages to Calicoon or below. There are good camping sites along the way, and with a companion who likes the life an interesting trip should result.

My own preference is for wading and poking along the shore, experimenting with various lures and trying to figure out the vagaries of runs and eddies. Water that I have always liked lies west of Hankins, near Long Eddy. There Clarence Kessler and I have taken some fine smallmouths, and I have learned a little about the river.

The Delaware is probably typical of most of our Eastern bass streams, and what a fly fisherman learns there will serve him, with slight variations, on the upper Susquehanna, the Potomac, the Connecticut or wherever he fishes. As with any other form of sport, study and observation pay dividends.

Bass may not be quite as finicky as trout, but it is a mistake to assume that they are fools. Approach them clumsily in clear water, and you will see only wakes, left by badly scared fish. These same bass probably would have been receptive to a properly presented lure, fished by a cautious angler.

Whenever possible, I prefer to fish upstream, even when using a bucktail or other underwater lure. This method is doubly advantageous in clear water and bright weather, as a much closer approach to the fish is possible. I like to cast quartering to the direction of flow and let the fly swing with the current, either drifting naturally or retrieved in little jerks. In the majority of cases a fish will hook itself if the water is swift.

The river smallmouth is a lover of fast water, having lost somewhere in the course of its evolution the more contemplative disposition of its blood brother, the largemouth. When actually feeding, bass are inclined to lie at the edge of a boiling rip, if it be a productive food lane. From its station in the strong current it will dash out and seize a drifting insect or nymph with verve. If that insect happens to be what radio people refer to as "a reasonable facsimile," and it in turn is attached to your rod via leader and line, you are in luck. Or perhaps "luck" isn't the word after all, because if you are wise to the ways of bass you will know pretty well where to place your lure.

The study of water is one of the most interesting things about stream-fishing. An old-timer can usually tell you what spots look "fishy" and what places don't. He will automatically pass up areas which appear dead, and cast over what appear to be productive stretches. And he will generally be right, even though he is fishing the stream for the first time. Years of subconscious study have given him what amounts to another sense —a nose for fish.

The beginner may be well advised to spend considerable time in observation while he goes about his bass fishing. Casting a lure with a fairly heavy fly rod all day long can be disastrous to arm and wrist. And if the creel remains comparatively empty on top of it, the result is pretty discouraging.

When fishing a stream for the first time—whether bass or trout water—take plenty of time to look things over before starting in. Sit down quietly and have a smoke. Observe where the main current enters a pool; follow its course and see where it swirls back to form eddies. Now look for floating chips, leaves and straws and follow their drift watchfully. There are the food lanes along which fish will lie. Did you see a swirl down by that big rock where the current splits? It's time to tie on a lure and get to casting. Maybe a floater will take him.

Bass which are resting in the deeper pools and backwaters, though not definitely "lying out" in search of insects, may often be interested in a properly presented lure. In such a situation a fly-spinner rig or lightly dressed bucktail with heavy hook will often do business. You must cast well upstream and allow the lure to sink almost to the bottom, drifting slowly with the current. Then retrieve in little jerks by stripping quickly a few inches of line at a time with the left hand. It is a trick that often results in the capture of a big bass. But it is hard work without the thrill of fast-water fishing. If your inclinations parallel mine, you will leave these fish of the deep eddies to the bait caster or the live-bait fishermen, who can cover that beat with much less effort.

A good sturdy dry-fly rod will serve for bass fishing, provided it isn't too light. A 3½-ounce rod having ample backbone will, of course, lick a two-pound bass as readily as it will a trout of the same weight. But that's not all of the story. The trout fly rod was designed to cast a delicate fly weighing practically nothing. But a bass lure is another thing—especially a cork-bodied bug, feather minnow or spinner. Not only does it have weight, but it also offers air resistance, and these factors combine to put a heavy strain on the bamboo fibers. It is well known that casting, not playing fish, softens a rod.

Opinions differ, of course, but my inclination is not to use a rod for bass fishing unless it is at least 8½ feet in length and weighs somewhat over 4½ ounces, with ample backbone. If I were to choose a rod principally for the river bass, I would prefer to select one with a length of 9 feet, weighing about 5¾ ounces.

Leaders may be shorter than those used for trout fishing, and they should be heavier. I have tried many kinds over a period of years, but recently have settled on 6-pound-test nylon, in one piece without knots. It has proved ideal under all conditions.

The final destiny of any good game fish is the frying-pan or broiler. Occasionally you hear someone say that he doesn't care for bass as food. That may be due to the way they are prepared. In the first place, no fish can be at its best unless cared for properly from the moment it is caught. Black bass, especially smallmouths, are rather strong, having a distinctive odor which some describe as resembling wild celery. I have never got the connection, but they do have a peculiar, though not unpleasant, aroma possessed by no other fish. It is highly important to clean bass shortly after catching, wipe them free of slime and pack them in a fern-lined creel with ventilation.

Upon arriving home, skin the bass—do not scale them. The skin is apt to be rank and will impart an unpleasant taste to the flesh. A skinned bass is as mild as any other fish. Broil or fry in butter and serve with tartar sauce and cole slaw. The bones aren't particularly troublesome, especially if you have cut the fins *out*, not *off*, when cleaning the fish.

While you are alternately munching browned bass and sipping Sauterne, plan your next trip. If there were any doubt in your mind when you sat down, it will be removed before the meal is over!

Fly-rod artistry is built along the stretches of a small stream. An occasional session is good for every angler; it will teach him patience and humility.

Quiet Eddies

To EVEN THE MOST ENTHUSIASTIC trout angler there comes a time when the roar and turmoil of the big river become overpowering. After bucking a heavy current for days on end, a man becomes physically tired. Something happens to him mentally, too. Wading is hard work; it calls for bodily exertion beyond the average, and constant alertness. A dozen hazards surround each step—loose gravel, slippery rocks, sudden drop-offs, marl bottom, strong currents. Any of these factors, if disregarded, can instantly put a man in a ticklish position.

After fishing a stream like the lower Beaverkill, the Delaware or the Manistee on several successive days, I become noticeably keyed up and nervous. And I have observed this condition in others. The lure of the big river is strong. To a greater extent than is true on smaller streams it is the home of the sockdolager, that fabulous fish which must be folded a couple of times before he will go into the creel. We all want to land him, of course, and though we seldom do it is comforting to know that on the big water we have a distinct chance.

125

Take the Beaverkill in early June. There's a full head of water running, and the May-fly is on. You step into a pool like Lockwoods or Baxters and strip line to cast. Just the business of getting started.

Smash! A brown boils up in a rip ten yards away, takes a natural off the water and gives you a quick glimpse of his caudal. It is four inches broad. Your pulse leaps up to 90 r.p.m., prompted by the thumping of your heart which, you fancy, can be heard above the roar of the river.

You are off to a swell start now, I can assure you. Dozens of times you will cast over that trout, and if he does you the honor of ignoring every attempt you won't mind. For you are smitten with the spell of big water; the churning current is in your blood, and the hiss of plunging water has gone to your head. Maybe you will hook your tantalizing quarry. Then you will stumble, slip and slide over slick rocks and through uncertain depths to fetch up two hundred yards below, badly blown and trembling like an aspen leaf.

If fly and leader hold and a kindly fate smiles, you may net a three-pound brownie. You have won! Or have you?

Judging from my own experience, I'd say "No." For fishing big water where heavy trout lie contains the same excitement potential as grouse hunting. Once you get the germ in your blood, the only halting-point will be a turned ankle or a wrist so stiff and sore from constant casting that it can no longer function. Then it is time to seek the peace and calm of some unpretentious little stream and regain your perspective.

You can't really define a little stream. It's senseless to say that a brook becomes a river after it gets so many yards wide; some do, and some don't. It isn't a matter of physical measurements at all, but entirely a question of temperament. Some small rivers, or large brooks, are merely pocket editions of big water. They have fast, heavy current, treacherous ledges and rocks and slippery bottoms—all the disadvantages of the big river without its big fish.

Other streams never seem to grow up, even though, physically, their banks may be the distance of a long cast apart. They have slick glassy reaches, quiet eddies, gentle ripples and intriguing runs where trout lie out waiting for drifting food. They have reasonable bottoms where a man may wade without thinking about it. They are friendly and intimate, just the kind of water needed by the angler who is surfeited with the big river and needs, for a time, to come into closer contact with the calmer aspect of his sport.

Having found and recognized such a stream, the thoughtful man will now set about cultivating his new acquaintance. By starting right he can develop a warm and lasting friendship.

"Technique" is a cold sort of word, and I hesitate to use it. It infers mechanics, method and procedure—all dreadfully imposing terms which sort of throw you off balance. You can get so messed up in it that you may easily forget about fishing. Still, a certain amount of technique is necessary, and it must be adapted to the peculiar conditions of the small stream if a man is to get the most fun out of his adventures.

To begin with, lay aside the long, heavy rod. Perhaps you have been using an 8½- or 9-footer, weighing 4½ to 6 ounces. It came in handy on the big water, where frequently you had to stretch out across a pool and lay a fly under a far bank; or eat into a wind that curled your line up like a garter snake. Here you won't need such a powerful stick. Short casts will be the rule, and accuracy counts more than distance. An 8-foot rod weighing 3½ to 4 ounces is ideal. It should, of course, have ample backbone, for a soft whippy rod is an abomination and useless for anything save catching pan-fish.

Leaders should be long and fine. Nine-foot gut or nylon leaders are preferable to shorter ones, and you will need them with both 3X and 4X points. Splice a loop in the end of the line for attaching the leader so that you can shorten the line to the proper length for netting a fish. The ordinary knot will, of course, jam against the top guide and get you in trouble.

Delicate flies are most effective for the shy trout of small streams. Here is an excellent chance for using some of the off-the-track patterns that you have been buying from time to time without knowing exactly why. Types which I have always liked are spentwings, quills, spiders and bivisibles. The most useful sizes are 12's and 14's, but I would never think of venturing out on any little river or large brook without a few 16's.

Much more important than tackle is the vital matter of tactics. How good are you at sneaking? Can you wade quietly, without stirring up long wakes in the water? Are you observant in such things as marking the position of the sun in order

Rainbow in the Rips

to keep your shadow off the water; in bending down low when approaching a pool where trout are lying out? If not, you will have to cultivate such methods, for on the small stream trout are ready to flee at the shadow of a passing heron.

Then there is the business of casting. Out on the big river you usually have unlimited space behind you and don't have to worry about your back cast. You can fish all day, with no holds barred, and will rarely get in trouble. For that very reason, many of us get sloppy in our casting and fail to keep the line up high, behind, where it belongs. A back cast that sags too low means an uncertain and wavering forward cast. It's like trying to build a house on a weak foundation—the ridge will soon buckle.

Fishing a wooded stream should be "required reading," every so often, for the fellow who finds himself dropping loops of line on the water with a fish-scaring *swoosh* when he really intended to lay out an easy and noiseless cast. The small water just won't stand it.

Brushy shores, overhanging limbs, boulders and ledges in the stream bed—seldom is there more than a few feet of clearance. A carelessly directed fly seems to take a special delight in attaching itself to the very top of an alder branch, ten feet beyond possible reach. If you pull, the leader will break. You can't climb the alder; it is too fragile. What do you say?

Sure, I say it too. And when I get through presenting my compliments to that alder—and its ancestors for several generations back—I resolve to be more careful. Sometimes it lasts for fully an hour! But such incidents do teach you caution.

When fishing a brushy stream, you must make up your mind to be confronted constantly by hazards. Determine to be calm; you will succeed part of the time. The rewards which the little stream has to offer are well worth any effort you make. You can, by diligent application, acquire skill that will surprise you.

Since keeping out of trouble depends largely upon how well you cast, it pays to add some tricks to your bag, if it does not already contain them. Almost first in importance is developing a working knowledge of the switch or roll cast. It is described and diagrammed in every practical book on fishing

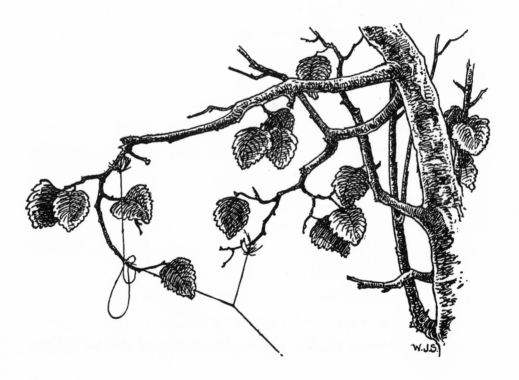

ever written. It was probably discovered by the first gent who ever used a fly rod, and was developed as a means of getting out of a jam in cases where there is no room for a back cast, but plenty of incentive to make one in the forward direction. There are lots of such cases, and always will be.

To make the roll cast, lay out about thirty feet of line and drop the rod tip down parallel to the water. Now start the rod going with a slowly accelerating movement backward and upward. Terminate the motion by flipping the tip sharply in a semicircle, ending abruptly in the direction of the cast. The line will follow through, lift off the water and flip forward dutifully in the approximate direction of your aim. It will lay out smoothly and quietly as you make progress. A good roll caster can easily handle forty feet or more of line, put his fly where he wants to, and do it with his back against a rocky cliff or brushy bank.

But fly-casting is an art in itself, and I can do no more here than to nibble at it. Before leaving the subject, I'd like to suggest two other casts which are invaluable to the angler who fishes small streams. They are the left-hand cast and the horizontal cast executed with the right hand across the body. These are priceless where one wades upstream along a right-hand bank with deep water in front but enticing riffles ahead which should be fished. If the shore is brushy, with no room for a normal back cast, either of these casts will take care of the situation—and practically nothing else will.

All the casting skill in the world, however, will get a man

nowhere unless he develops a certain sense which is peculiarly needed for success in fishing small waters. It must always be remembered that the closer you approach a trout the more chance there becomes of its seeing you. On the big river you are customarily casting forty to fifty feet of line, and you are well out of the trout's angle of vision. But the small stream shrinks distance and perspective. Before you know it, you may walk up to a run and have the humiliating experience of seeing a pound fish scoot for cover. A careful approach and a well-placed fly could easily have put that trout in your creel.

The first time I ever fished the upper stretch of the West Branch of the Croton, I came unexpectedly upon a beautiful pool. It had a perpendicular rocky bank on one side, shaded by a leaning hemlock. The water purled and rippled over a deep hole, and at the tail of the pool a glassy slick offered a perfect drift for a dry fly. The other bank, on which I crouched, was a flat, gravelly beach. There was ample room for a back cast and, thinking myself out of sight, I fished enthusiastically, covering every foot of the water.

Fifteen minutes of earnest effort were unrewarded, and I went on upstream puzzled, but not discouraged. Such a pool simply had to hold trout. My approach had been wrong; and while it was not apparent to me, I was probably visible to whatever fish were in the water.

In a couple of hours I cut back through the woods to a point below the pool and worked up to it, this time on the opposite side—the rocky bank. Completely hidden now, I dropped a fly in the tail of the pool and was instantly fast to a 12-inch native trout. I netted him downstream, out of sight, and returned to take two other nice fish before things got completely stirred up. It was a graphic demonstration of the value of concealment.

In May and early June, when streams are running bank-full and there are good hatches of aquatic insects on the water, catching trout on the small stream is not difficult. With reasonable caution a dry or a wet fly, even fairly presented, will coax a trout out from behind a rock or grassy bank. But when the heat of midsummer lies on the land and waters start to shrink, small-stream fishing becomes a science—and a most fascinating one. Then a man has to put all his wits and native caution to work; and if he can return from an afternoon's fishing with half a dozen plump trout in his creel, he has done well.

Under such conditions it is almost essential to fish upstream, particularly where the country is precipitous, as is so often the case in the East. Within the distance of an ordinary cast—twenty feet on a wooded brook—the stream will have dropped enough to make the angler plainly visible to the trout.

Often in warm weather trout will refuse to rise to the most tempting dry fly. This is especially true on bright days. Yet a delicate wet fly, fished upstream and drifted by them naturally, will bring results. They're like the fellow who is hungry, but is too doggoned lazy to go and get himself something to eat. This is a tip worth remembering.

When fishing a small stream in late summer during low water, the wise angler uses his eyes constantly. Trout will often be spotted at a considerable distance, lying out in search of food. They are invariably difficult to catch, but that is where the fun comes in. A careful plan must be made. Fly and leader should be readied in advance, and line stripped preparatory to casting with the minimum of movement.

Next, the stalk begins. Crouching behind a convenient boulder or bush, the angler slips forward, a step at a time. The cast must be perfect and the fly should drop softly, near the closest trout. If it comes off well and a good fish is hooked and landed, the performer can justly feel proud of himself. He has not only displayed his skill as an angler, but has demonstrated that his instincts for the chase have not been entirely dulled or bred out by civilization.

Don't let your late-summer fishing become a routine affair. Keep alert and observant. Take in everything and try to figure out where trout would lie in a given situation. Submerged logs, ledge rock, overhanging grassy banks and sunken roots are obvious hide-outs. Small brooks entering the main stream mean cool water, and if there is anything like a pool and cover at the junction the stage is set for the taking of a fish—or at least a good try.

Often a spring, trickling down from the side of a hill, will form a good-sized pool before narrowing down and emptying into the main stream. The water is clear as crystal and usually shaded. It is rare not to find a sizable school of trout in such a place. If properly worked, a spring hole can turn out to be a treasure trove. I can think of half a dozen such fascinating spots in the Catskills, and at times they have retrieved what otherwise would have been a practically blank day.

Once, while fishing the East Branch of the Delaware for smallmouths, I came upon a spring pool a hundred feet long, with considerable width. I spotted a good brown trout lying in three feet of water about twenty feet from shore. The bottom was sandy, with a few small rocks scattered here and there. The trout lay quietly fanning the water, apparently with not a care in the world.

We had a guest at the house, and he had expressed a desire for trout. It was hot and late in the season; so this item of fare was not easily come by. The fish before me looked like a good pounder; I needed him badly and therefore took some pains in plotting his downfall.

Searching through my fly box, I selected a dun-colored palmer, hackled with Scotch grouse. It was an English wet fly, tied on a No. 14 Hall's turn-up eye hook and looked remarkably like a spider. I knotted it to a 9-foot 4X Hardy leader, rubbed both fly and leader with mud to make them sink, and cast carefully a yard beyond the trout.

Allowing some time for the fly to sink, I retrieved it with little twitches. It passed the old boy's nose looking, I thought, pretty convincing. But he didn't agree with me. And his opinion was all that mattered. Two more attempts brought the same result; so I rested the case. In the meantime the trout dozed on contentedly.

In ten minutes I tried again, this time changing tactics.

Maybe he would fall for the old English poachers' trick. I cast just over him and jockeyed the fly into such a position that it settled to the bottom about three inches from his nose. Laying the rod down carefully, I had a smoke.

Fully five minutes were allowed to pass before I picked it up again. Then, by twitching the line the slightest bit with the left hand, the fly was wiggled along the sandy bottom. The movement caused the hackles to expand and contract, like an insect moving its legs. This interested the old boy—definitely. He swung around and stared hard. I stopped fiddling with the fly. He stopped and thought it over.

Encouraged by his what-have-we-here attitude, I inched the fly along again. This time I thought I could detect his mouth watering. It was getting too good to spoil; so I halted once more. Now he was like a cat watching a mouse-hole. Fins fanning the water excitedly, that brownie was ready to pounce. A couple of quick twitches and a three-inch jerk, then *wham!* He had it well back in his mouth.

He put up a swell scrap and proved to be a 14-inch 1-pound fish, as estimated. Really, that trout should have been released, but you can't fry sentiment and serve it to a guest who is depending on you to come across. He wouldn't understand.

It has occurred to me that, in reading the above incident, some pure soul might be deeply shocked, considering the method to be unsportsmanlike. Let me recommend that such a sensitive person try it and find out for himself. I would suggest a nice muggy day, with the temperature around 85 degrees, a cloud of ravenous mosquitoes ready and willing to pounce, and a liberal garnish of nettles swishing about the face and hands. These are fairly constant properties of most spring holes. If, after standing immobile for minutes at a time under such conditions and, with luck, taking a trout or two, the critic still thinks it's unfair to the fish, I'll eat his catch raw!

Seriously, the poachers' method is just a stunt, and one requiring great patience. It was shown to me by an old game warden, who brought it over from the other side. I wouldn't believe it would work until I had it proved. It will never seriously reduce the fish population—in this country or elsewhere.

An entire book could be devoted to the topic of how to fish the small stream. But I doubt that it would benefit either the writer or the reader a great deal. One needs but a few hints— the rest he will find out for himself. And that is as it should be.

In the final summing up, angling is an adventure, and we should always regard it as such. What we fish with and where —whether on river or brook—how many trout we creel, and how much water we cover matters little. It is what we see, feel, learn and experience that counts. That, after all, is why we fish.

Contrary to popular belief, I have always entertained the quaint notion that the fellow who pans gold in some turbulent stream gets a bigger kick out of the yellow metal than the financier who owns quantities of it and can spend it lavishly.

The gold-hunter gets a thrill out of every scoop; at any moment he may turn up a valuable nugget, and that is high adventure. The plutocrat gets gout.

Every trout stream, every bass and salmon river in the land, is lined with gold. It is up to us as anglers to find it. The nuggets do not consist only of big fish or full creels. There are other good and valuable considerations.

In writing these chapters I hope I have not dwelt too much on theory and method. To a beginner, some of it is necessary. But once learned, it should become subconscious. Only in that way can a man become free to absorb impressions and be ready for adventure.

The gold you will find on the stream is inexhaustible—in fact, the deeper you tap the vein the richer it becomes. That is one of the delightful paradoxes of our sport, which, come to think of it, is full of contradictions all along the line.

Perhaps, in the final check-up, that is why anglers are different—a little wacky, but proud of it!

OF THIS EDITION
ONE THOUSAND COPIES WERE
PRINTED IN
MAY 1970